What Others Are Saying About

A HEART FOR ADVENTURE

"As a young man I thought God wanted me to comb my hair, dress nice, and sit quietly. Through life, story, and God's word this book invites all of us to live out amazing adventures with the Author of all adventure. Jimmy and Bob live large for God and remind us that abundant life doesn't begin when we die, it begins when we receive. God has invited us on the adventure, and these men serve as two of His tour guides. You should probably buckle up for the ride."

—TOM ANTHONY
Owner/President: IMMI (Indiana Mill Manufacturing, Inc)

"Jimmy and Bob's ability to communicate the love Christ has for us is made clear, understandable, and interesting in *A Heart for Adventure*. This is more than a devotional, it's a great read to assist you in your walk regardless of where you are in your relationship with God."

—CRAIG MORGAN
Country Music Artist

"The cougar story, one of fifty adventure stories within these pages, is worth more than the price of this book. Riveting, to the point, and directly on target for how we all need to live our lives in the face of temptation. An important read for all men, especially in these times."

—JIM CAVIEZEL
Movie and TV Actor, Played Jesus in Mel Gibson's Passion of The Christ

"When we go on adventures with Jimmy or a man like Bob, we always return home feeling spiritually enriched. It's both time in the bush and time in the Word, hunting and worshipping together. Just doesn't get any better!"

—BEVERLY PENA
CFO of TTG Utilities, LP

"Most people spend their time making money, when they should be spending their money making time to be with their families! This book encouraged me to work harder to put my family time first, and trust God to make my workplace as fruitful as He intends it to be."

—MARK AMMERMAN
Global Energy Banking, Scotiabank

"These guys hit the target about the important issues of living life well."
—MIKE HUCKABEE
44th Governor of Arkansas, Host of Huckabee, *Fox News Channel*

"Follow Bob and Jimmy's advice and you will live a fuller, more rewarding life, and when you look back it won't be with regret but with pleasure."
—DAVID KEENE
President, National Rifle Association

"The works of Jimmy Sites not only awaken the spirit of adventure, but bring us closer to God through the experience. There is no greater inspirational writer for the Christian outdoorsman."
—JOHN CARTER CASH
Oscar and Grammy Winner, Son of Johnny and June Carter Cash

"*A Heart for Adventure* is full of touching stories of folks seeking their true selves, wanting to discover their soul in the great outdoors. Many have tried to tie in nature to self-revelation, but few hit the 'heart' of the matter. Jimmy and Bob do that in spades and draw us in to what the real Creator intended for us. These stories are riveting, the locations incomparable and the revelations revealing."
—ROCKY MCELVEEN
Alaska Big Game Guide, Inspirational Speaker,
and Best-selling Author of Wild Men, Wild Alaska

"Guided by the Hand and Word of God, Jimmy brings a unique perspective to all of his adventures that stops you in your tracks and makes you think. Entertaining and insightful."
—JOHN ANDRETTI
Race Car Driver

"As a friend and hunting partner of these two great sportsmen, I encourage you to discover the adventure and life lessons they share in this book. Jimmy and Bob guide us to a better understanding of how God speaks to us in the still of the morning hunt, or in the middle of a rushing trout stream, and help us take aim at the target of Christ-centered living."
—TOM SCOTT, PRESIDENT/COO
Sky Angel/Fave TV Network

"Jimmy and Bob have a God-given ability to see and communicate biblical truths in seemingly ordinary events."
—REX MURRAY
Owner: Ringneck Country,
14-Time National Champion Vizsla Dog Breeder/Trainer

A HEART for ADVENTURE

LIVING A LIFE ON TARGET

Bob Reccord & Jimmy Sites

Dedication

From Bob Reccord

I dedicate this work to the man whom, when I met Him, radically changed my life and has given me an amazing ride—Jesus Christ. And I express my love and devotion to the woman who helps me celebrate life to the fullest, has been an incredible partner for over four decades, and supports me in my passion for life and the outdoors—Cheryl.

From Jimmy Sites

I dedicate this book to the ones who first instilled within me the love of God and the love of the outdoors—my parents—Carroll and Sarah Loreta Sites. I also thank my best friend and companion in the ultimate life adventure called marriage—Amanda. And the arrows in my quiver that have made life so much fun for over two decades—my kids—Christin, Mary, and Jonathan.

Special Thanks

We would like to express our sincere thanks to an incredible craftsman with words, our editor Lawrence Kimbrough. To Brandon Chesbro, thanks for some great photographs and an eye-catching cover design. Amanda Sites, your artistic drawings inside the book add so much, thank you! To Katherine Lloyd, your typesetting and graphic layout skills are top-shelf. Kyle Olund, thank you for your generous instruction and guidance. And finally, to all of our friends who have journeyed with us on the adventures within this book, our dust-covered hats are off to you. You all make a great team!

Table of Contents

Introduction

MEET YOUR OUTFITTERS

Outfitters can be helpful partners and guides in many fishing and hunting adventures. Their experience and judgment come in handy, serving to maximize the journey and make any outing a success. Their mission and focus is to help the outdoor enthusiast do his or her very best, take advantage of every opportunity, and hopefully become better at the end of the trip than at the beginning.

Two men who are seasoned outdoor veterans as well as trained theologians have come together to serve as your outfitters through the pages of this book. So meet your outfitters:

DR. BOB RECCORD has been a business executive, a senior pastor in three states, and the founding president of one of the nation's largest mission agencies. During both 9/11 and hurricanes Katrina, Rita, and Wilma, he oversaw one of the nation's largest disaster relief programs. He has also worked in Washington, D.C., with key influencers and conservative leaders in government, business, higher education, and media for the promotion of traditional values and calling America back to its founding principles. Between 2006 and 2012, Bob spoke to more than 210,000 men through his *Total Life Impact Ministries*. In May 2013, he served as keynote speaker of the NRA National Prayer Breakfast in Houston, Texas. He writes regularly as a Master Sportsman for the *Christian Sportsman's Fellowship* magazine, and has also authored nine books including the best-selling book *Beneath the Surface*, with over 250,000 copies in print. Bob and his wife, Cheryl, lead marriage conferences across the nation, and Bob speaks frequently on behalf of crisis pregnancy care centers from coast to coast, raising hundreds of thousands of dollars to protect life. Loving adventure, Bob has paraglided off the Swiss Alps, gone scuba diving with his son among sharks, and hunted across the nation, as well as multiple times in Africa. He has three grown children and two grandchildren.

 **DR. JIMMY SITES** once served as the preaching minister for a Nashville church of several thousand members, but for more than a decade has been producing and hosting one of the longest-running and top-rated outdoor television shows in the nation. The award-winning *Spiritual Outdoor Adventures with Jimmy Sites* airs weekly in 75 million households on various networks. He has lived in the Amazon jungle with a Stone Age Indian tribe, explored beneath pyramids in Egypt, been stranded by a winter storm in the deep woods of Canada, copiloted a fighter jet pulling six g's, driven

fourteen laps in an Indy car on the Charlotte Motor Speedway, and been stranded in the wilderness of Alaska by a broken bush plane. Jimmy has harvested more than twenty-three species of game animals with a bow. And in 2010, he and his team won the Big Buck Outdoor Games, competing against twenty of the nation's leading professional hunters and producers. Jimmy is also a professional speaker and best-selling author. He helped edit the *Heart of the Outdoors* Bible and has given away more than $1.25 million worth of Bibles to TV viewers, children, prisoners, and many others. He is a spokesperson for Christian Bowhunters of America, Centershot, and Compassion International, and is even an animated character, along with Hunter Ed and Buddy Buck, in cartoons that teach outdoor-related safety and ethics to children. He and his wife, Amanda, have three children—Christin, Mary, and Jonathan.

A Note from Your Guides

ood guides share from their own experiences, both successes and failures. They are constantly on the lookout not only to protect their clients, but also to help them achieve their goals and make lasting memories. Good guides love to share their skills with the people they serve and help them grow in their own abilities as outdoorsmen.

That is what we want for you through the pages of this book. We are inviting you to go on some adventures with us. Trust us, we will be transparent. You will see our strengths and our weaknesses. Our Outfitter's Handbook will be the Word of God. It is God's *Owner's Manual,* written to help us become everything God created us to be. It is essential in guiding us along the steep paths and dangerous cliffs of life. It keeps us safe when passing through the dark jungles. And it is an invaluable map or GPS that will ultimately lead us home for eternity.

If you don't believe in that kind of stuff, at least give this book a try. Save your judgment of its contents until the end.

If you are a believer, get ready to grow. We address some personal issues throughout, as seen in some very wild stories, and you will be asked at the end of each chapter to interact with what you read and with God's Word. We'll also introduce you to the concept of what we call "breath prayers," little statements of trust, worship, and commitment to God that can become part of your ongoing conversation with Him. One of these will appear at the end of each chapter, just to give you the idea and to spark new breath prayers of your own. Our ultimate desire is that you become a fully surrendered follower of Jesus Christ and impact your world because of His work in and through you.

With that said, it's time to gear up for living a life on target. Lace up your boots, strap on your backpack, grab your weapon, and let's start the adventure. Here we go . . .

Yours *on mission,*   Ready to hit the trail,

(Gandalf) "I am looking for someone to share in an adventure that I am arranging, and it's very difficult to find anyone."

(Mr. Baggins) "I should think so — in these parts! We are plain quiet folk and have no use for adventures. Nasty disturbing uncomfortable things! Make you late for dinner!"

—J.R.R. Tolkien, *The Hobbit*

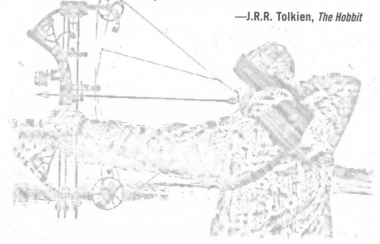

"Life is either a daring adventure or nothing."
—Helen Keller, *Laura Moncur's Motivational Quotations*

Bob

REDISCOVERED PASSIONS

When I consider your heavens, the work of your fingers, the moon and the stars, which you have set in place, what is man that you are mindful of him? (Psalm 8:3–4)

The predawn, December Georgia air made me glad I was alive and enjoying the health to be heading toward the woods with my bow. The frosty morning tree line felt like welcoming arms wrapping around me as I reveled in the call of the owl, the honking of geese gliding into a perfect touchdown, and a distant coyote's howl.

Quietly waiting for the dawn to make its long awaited entrance, I caught myself reflecting backward to another set of crisp mornings a few years prior, perched in an enclosed deer stand on my friend's south Texas acreage. Orange and purple hues were creeping like fingers over the eastern horizon. In the shadows, deer could be vaguely seen moving in the distance, cautious and hesitant, wondering if their forward steps would be safe ones . . . or vulnerable ones. My inner being was screaming, "Oh man, how I love this! I was born to do this!"

But if that's so, then why had I only found myself loving it in the last ten years?

I had grown up as an only adopted child in southern Indiana. Both parents had been raised in southern Illinois during the Great Depression, and neither had been able to finish high school. Familiar with the all too common fear of having too much month left over at the end of their money, my dad took on the honorable challenge of working two jobs—toiling in the construction trade during the week, and then running a small, family-owned Illinois farm most weekends.

During some of those weekends, I remember taking out my BB gun and heading to the fields. I learned how to treat guns with respect and to value the experience of the hunt. I spent hours in the woods, working on my aim. Striving to move with stealth. Studying the habits of wildlife. Dreaming of being a successful hunter!

My biggest thrills of all, however, were when Dad would pull down the .22 rifle and work with me on my shots. That was the big leagues! The handful of times he took me rabbit or quail hunting with the 12-guage were beyond words! I remember my first rabbit—a crowning achievement fit for a king! That's exactly how I felt—like the King of the World!

But those times were a rarity. Most of the hunting and fishing I did weren't with Dad. He was always working too hard. Too busy. And honestly, I can respect that. He was a good provider. A faithful, sacrificial husband and father. No doubt his diligent example is what has given me a work ethic that's served me well in life. But time alone with him—just Dad and me—was hard to come by. I'm not sure, frankly, that he ever quite realized how highly I valued my time alone with him. I was just left to assume he wasn't all that interested in it . . . in being with me.

So I buried my love for hunting and fishing. And somewhere along the way, it just lost its allure. The thrill was gone. And life went on.

In the ensuing years, I had my own kids—two daughters and a son. And I found myself working hard to provide for the family, fulfill my work obligations, travel as a speaker, and do everything required of me. Then later on, when my own son expressed some interest in hunting, I found myself—like my dad—too busy to break away. The same great experiences I had missed with my father, I was now beginning to miss with my son as well.

Thankfully, about ten years ago I rediscovered my absolute *love* for the outdoors, through an invitation by a friend to come hunt on his Texas ranch. During that first reintroduction to the woods, I harvested a deer and two turkeys. My thrill registered off the Richter scale! And I was hooked once again with the zeal I had experienced as a kid.

But this time, I determined that I wasn't going to experience it alone. My son would be a part of my hunting life as much as he wanted, any time he desired. And I've been true to that mission ever since.

I will take to my grave the memory of that next year, when not two hours after returning to my friend's ranch, Bryan brought down an amazing eight-point buck. I admit, I can get pretty juiced whenever I harvest an animal or haul in an impressive fish. But I have never been more excited than watching my son claim such a prize for himself.

And I've often wondered, "What took me so long to get my priorities in the proper order?"

How about you? Do you have a son or daughter, grandson or

granddaughter, who's hoping you would spend more time with them? Are you investing in the next generation and cultivating their love for the outdoors? Are you teaching them the rules of fair chase? Do they know the thrill of pulling in that fighting fish because they learned it at your side? Have you sat at the base of a tree together with your two hearts racing, calling in that Tom? Has the pounding of wings shot through you like electricity as you and your child acquired the target of the flushing covey or rising pheasant?

When you engage in this kind of quality time, it opens up the opportunity for those important conversations. About character and spiritual values. About wise decision making. About so many vital things. And it can happen in the most outstanding classroom possible—God's breathtaking creation!

If these experiences are true of you, *great job!* If not, why not start now?

Remember, it's not too late to live a life that matters . . . starting right where you live.

⊕ Taking Aim

1. What could you do to increase your kid's/grandkid's love for the outdoors?

2. What are you letting become more important to you than time spent alone with them?

3. Is there an old passion or interest you've allowed to get buried under a busy life? How could you seek to recapture it . . . and perhaps share it with your kids or grandkids?

- - -

Lord, help me see what really matters.

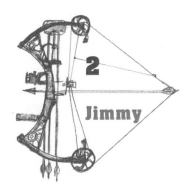

2

Jimmy

THE SEARCH FOR MY HEART

Above all else, guard your heart, for everything you do flows from it. (Proverbs 4:33)

Goodland, Kansas, is home to some great pheasant hunting. A few miles from town lives a man named Rex Murray. Rex is a world-renowned dog breeder and trainer, particularly with the vizsla breed of pointers (pronounced VEEZ-luh). Rex and his dogs have won numerous national championships and competed at the world level. His vizslas truly are amazing animals!

My first trip to hunt with Rex included several of my friends. Bluegrass musician Ricky Skaggs was with us, excited to get into some pheasant action. And with more than 7,000 acres of prime habitat to work with, we knew Rex would be taking us to many locations that held birds, each with its own unique landscape.

We started out in an area called Little South Dakota, featuring a cut cornfield to the right, bordered by a grown-up ditch to the left, where the walking was fairly tough through the waist-high grass and tangled briars.

When we relocated to Rooster Draw, I saw a drain with an inclining hill on both sides covered with knee-high grass. It was very open, dotted by only a small number of briar patches. The walking was easy there, and we could see a long ways. This was a great location to watch the dogs work.

We finished up at The Hole, and true to its name, it literally wore us out. The area looked like a huge bowl of several hundred acres that had grown up into one massive thicket with pockets of low grass here and there. It was by far the toughest bird hunting terrain I have ever traversed.

Here's my point (no pun intended). No matter what the terrain was like, whether extremely difficult or a cakewalk through the park, those vizsla dogs were just happy to be there doing what God created them to do. They love it so much! As soon as Rex would walk toward their pens, ready to pick out the lucky dogs that were going to head out on the day's excursion with him, they were shaking with excitement, whimpering uncontrollably. When he let them out of the dog trailer at the location where we were about to hunt, they hit the ground running. Their noses were on the ground almost before their feet were. When Rex would call them in after being in the field for a while, wanting to offer them a drink, they would obey, lap their water, and then immediately go right back out searching for the next pheasant.

They listened to their master and obeyed orders well. They honored each other when on point. They retrieved the dead birds gently without biting the breast meat. They disregarded their aching muscles and the many cuts inflicted by the briars. They were fully immersed in being exactly what God intended them to be.

Their hearts belonged completely to Rex and to the hunt. I believe they would have died in the field before they'd have dreamed of letting up.

I've done a good bit of thinking about the hearts of those dogs. It's caused me to take a long look at my own heart as well. Do I love God as much as those dogs love Rex and the hunt? Am I as sold out to God as I should be? Do I really love Him with all my heart, soul, mind, and strength? Am I immersed in being exactly what God intends me to be?

Many other things in life have competed for my heart. Many battles have taken place over the years. And though I have often ended up the worse for wear after some of these contests, I can say with confidence that my heart now belongs to the One to whom it should belong—my heavenly Father. And by leading my heart to believe on the Lord Jesus, He has placed within me a *new* heart, beating to the rhythm and pulse of His grace.

And so I walk in peace as a result. I journey for a different reason. No matter how difficult or easy the terrain of life, I simply go wherever God sends me for whatever He wants of me. I don't have to be the one who picks the hunting location. I don't have to worry about whether or not there will be any pheasants when I get there. I can just trust when my Master calls, and I can enjoy ample drinks from His living water. I keep on doing what He created me to do even when injured or tired. I honor others who are on the journey with me. I don't have to question anything my Master assigns me to do, and I don't have to know why I'm being asked to do it. I just have to go . . . to be available with a heart that is pure and open, ready to beat its last beat for the Father.

Can your heart say the same?

 **Taking Aim**

1. A religious scholar asked Jesus one day, "What is the greatest commandment?" Read Jesus' answer found in Mark 12:30.

2. How would you define the difference between the four things mentioned by Jesus in his answer?

3. On a scale of 1 (worst) to 10 (best), rate the spiritual condition of your heart right now:

   1—2—3—4—5—6—7—8—9—10

4. If you are not satisfied with your rating above, what do you plan to do to increase the health rating of your spiritual heart?

- - -

Lord, create in me a new heart.

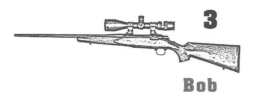

3

Bob

THE STINK WILL TELL THE STORY

You may be sure that your sin will find you out. (Numbers 32:23)

W e had just finished one of the most memorable South Dakota pheasant hunts I had ever experienced. The weather had been nice and cool, but not a frigid icebox like I had experienced before. We felt good walking the fields, with coats comfortably open, as someone yelled, "Rooster!" and we had swung into action, knocking a lot of birds out of the sky.

Now the time to return to the daily grind had arrived. Goodbyes had been expressed, slaps on the back, parting handshakes had been exchanged, and most everyone was gone. I was the last to say my final thank-you to our host, Paul Nelson, who runs one of the most amazing pheasant hunting operations I have ever seen. Paul had become a friend over several years of shared experience, and I always wished I could take a bit of the ambience and warmth with me as I left.

But since I couldn't, Paul suggested the next best thing: taking home some pheasant.

I had looked into how much it cost to FedEx or UPS frozen pheasant to my home in Georgia, and it rivaled the national debt! Explaining this to Paul and his team, they came up with a better idea. Since I was flying to Minneapolis, changing planes, and flying straight to Atlanta, I could just put the hard, frozen birds in my suitcase and simply remove them when I got home. They were so well frozen, there would be no problem.

That was before the plane leaving Pierre, South Dakota, was late, thereby cutting my time extremely tight in Minneapolis. Fearing I would miss my next plane and be stuck overnight, I did my best version of an open-field run through the Minneapolis airport before breathing a deep sigh of relief as I collapsed into my seat, ready for takeoff. I was going to make it.

My suitcase, however, wasn't so lucky.

Not seeing my suitcase (loaded with frozen pheasant) circling around the conveyor belt upon my arrival, I made my way sheepishly to baggage service and expressed my dilemma. They assured me that my bag should come in on the next flight. But by the next morning, it *still* hadn't arrived. Or by the following afternoon . . . evening. Or even by the morning after that.

By this time, I was frantic. What about the pheasant? I was betting they weren't frozen *that* hard!

When I called the next morning, the airlines confessed that the baggage was evidently lost. And that's when I was forced to make a little confession of my own. The missing piece of luggage, I assured them, should not be hard to locate. In just a short while, if they hadn't been able to find it with their eyes, they would find it with their noses. Not only would airline personnel know where it was, but every dog in the city would know. The stink would tell the story!

That's how life works. When something is hidden where it shouldn't be, it will inevitably be found out because the "stink" will become obvious, regardless of how well we may think we've hidden it. Just ask Gen. David Petraeus, Arnold Schwarzenegger, Bill Clinton, Bernie Madoff, and a host of other well-known examples. Or go back several years and look into the lives of King David, Judas Iscariot, Ananias and Sapphira, or even further back to where it all began, with Adam and Eve.

We may *think* something is packed away, hidden, secure, or sufficiently buried so that no one will ever know. But it will always come to the surface. It's not a matter of *if* but *when*.

So as you look into your own life, is there anything you've packed away, covered over, or hidden away, deep enough that you think—you hope—it will never come to light? Have you tried to just forget about it? Are you hoping you'll never have to deal with it again?

Just remember, your sins will find you out.

Too often, we see this truism as somehow a punishment from God. But in doing so, we actually miss His primary purpose and motivation in allowing our hidden sin to become public. Our heavenly Father knows that as long as our sin is hidden, we will try to convince ourselves and others that we have it all together. But the Father has a bigger plan in mind. He is at work conforming us to become more like Christ. And He knows that only by exposing our stinky little secrets can we truly experience what Jesus said when he declared, "I have come that they may have life, and have it to the full" (John10:10). Only when that hidden sin becomes public—and we discover He loves us anyway—can we truly understand what God's love is really all about.

What action do you need to take so you can head off that hidden sin at the pass? Is there a sin to confess? Is there an apology to make? Forgiveness to request? A correction to make?

The ball is in your court. But don't wait too long or too late. Because you'll soon be starting to stink.

⊕ Taking Aim

1. Would you be so bold as to pray these words from Psalm 139? "Search me, O God, and know my heart; test me and know my anxious thoughts. See if there is any offensive way in me, and lead me in the everlasting way" (verses 23–24).

2. Why is it so hard and threatening for us to pray a prayer like that?

3. When was the last time God's conviction put His finger on something in your life that you knew He wanted you to change? Did you do it?

4. Have you been dwelling on certain things that you know are displeasing to God? Doing things? Saying things? *Not* doing things? Today is the best day to start making these things right.

- - -

Lord, get the stink out.

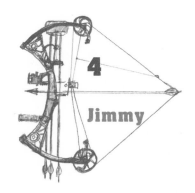

4

Jimmy

COUGAR ON THE PROWL

No temptation has overtaken you except what is common to mankind. And God is faithful; he will not let you be tempted beyond what you can bear. But when you are tempted, he will also provide a way out so that you can endure it.
(1 Corinthians 10:13)

anging up the phone, I jumped straight out of my chair, shouting and fist-pumping the air in my office, not really caring if anyone could see me. I had just been invited to New Mexico to hunt a rogue cougar that had killed hundreds of elk and mule deer and who now was killing for sport. This cougar was a master at avoiding hunters and trappers, currently roaming a rugged mountain range on the New Mexico-Colorado border. This was an old, female cat. Very large. And very dangerous.

I was elated. I'd be going with the top cougar guide in New

Mexico along with two of his track dogs, and I would be allowed to hunt this bloodthirsty beast with a bow.

Pretty exciting.

Since you can order the video of this amazing adventure from my office or Web site, I won't take time here to repeat all the mile-high details of the hunt. There are too many to tell. I'll only summarize by saying it was one of the hardest things I have ever done, made doubly hard by the extremely cold temperatures and deep snow. And when I finally harvested that cat with an arrow, I was overwhelmed—surprised, really—by my various emotions. I literally came to tears.

Part of my reaction post-kill, I think, was related to the respect I felt for the cougar. She was a killing machine. That cat had stalked many animals much larger than herself, taking them down by jumping on her victim's back, biting its neck. The captured animal would fall to the ground, unable to move, leaving its soft belly in perfect position for being peeled open by the back claws of the cougar. She would then go for the warm, beating heart. Death and conquest.

Just the thought made me shudder. It still does. Even now, whenever I pass beside the full body mount of that very cougar, frozen in stalking position, looking down at me with her menacing gaze from the roof of a trapper's cabin inside my lodge, I can still get an occasional spine tingle.

This past summer, however, I felt that same kind of tingle again. In a much different setting. From a much different cougar.

I was in Oklahoma City, having spoken the night before at a wild game supper sponsored by Crossings Community Church. I awoke bright and early in my hotel and went down to the fitness room around 6:30. Four other men and women were already in there working out when I arrived, but an elliptical was open, so I hopped on and set it for thirty minutes. By the time I stepped off the machine a half hour later, everyone had left the room.

Given the time and space, I decided to do a few lifting exercises before heading back upstairs to shower. And no sooner had I started this slow wind-down than an attractive, middle-aged woman entered the room to begin her own workout.

I said hello when she entered. She did the same. Nothing more was said for about ten minutes. Then rather suddenly, she paused between sets and asked, "So what brings you to Oklahoma City?" I looked up and told her I'd come to town for a wild game supper event the previous night.

"So you ate wild animals there?" she asked.

"Yes," I answered. "It's what we eat at home as well."

To this she replied, "I own seven butcher shops in my home state. Can I purchase wild game meat to sell?"

"No," I said, explaining that it's illegal to sell the meat from wild animals without a permit.

That's when she asked me a question I get from a lot of people: "What's your favorite wild animal to eat?" It's a question I answer the exact same way every time: "I've always thought of Axis deer as the best . . . that is, until recently." People can never leave that statement just sitting there without asking the next logical question: "And what did you have that's better than Axis deer?"

I always pause and smile when I answer.

"Cougar."

I don't know, that response just always surprises people. It never fails to generate a "wow" or "I didn't know you could eat cat meat." I've given that same answer to that same question and gotten the same response dozens and dozens of times. But I know something else: sometimes I am as naïve as a brick. And I never expected to turn this whole little discussion into a whole different direction.

When I said the word "cougar" to this woman, a transformation took place unlike any I have ever seen before. She basically turned into the same kind of killing-machine beast that I'd hunted in the snowy mountains of New Mexico. She began to slink toward me, eyes with vertical pupils, narrowing with every inch as she advanced. It was as if her fingernails had turned into claws. And before she could even ask the next question, I could feel the hair standing up on the back of my neck.

She purred the words, "Do you mean the wild animal? Or a hot, wild woman like me?"

I promise I'm not making this up. I was so stunned by what was happening, my jaw dropped wide open. My tongue must have been paralyzed by her words, like it was coated with frog poison from the Amazon. I couldn't speak. I just began to mutter sounds. And began backing up.

But that didn't stop the approach of cat woman. Her intentions were crystal clear.

"So are you here for the day?"

Feeling cornered, I finally found my tongue again. (I guess the cat had it for a moment.) "My plane flies out at noon," I said, the words sounding like my mouth was full of marbles.

But that didn't stop her. "How about postponing your flight until tomorrow and let's have some fun?"

Now what's a guy to do at a moment like this?

The Bible says to "flee," as in "flee from sexual immorality" (1 Corinthians 6:18). And that's just what I did. On instinct. Without saying another word, I turned and walked briskly out of the room.

Escaped the cougar's lair.

Gathering speed as I run-walked toward my hotel room, I whipped out my cell phone and called my wife, who didn't answer. (I left her a flustered message, something about a cougar attack.) I then dialed the number of my hosting minister there in Oklahoma, who was scheduled to take me to the airport later that morning. He didn't answer either, so I left a message for him as well: "Mike, I know you're not supposed to pick me up until 9:30, but I need you to come get me *right now!* I'll be in the lobby." I didn't even take time to shower. I just packed my bags and sat downstairs sweating bullets until Mike picked me up.

What did I learn from this?

First, I learned not to talk about cougars around middle-aged women. Second, I learned that women in our society today are more aggressive in asking for sex. And third, I learned something about me. I do have the power to say no, but it is really not a power of my own as much as it is the power of God in me.

If my saying no to sex with a beautiful woman is based on my own power, there will likely come a time in my life when I will mess up. I'm not always on my A-game spiritually. Sometimes I'm exhausted and not thinking very clearly. Even though my wife is awesome, sometimes our marriage goes through rough waters for various reasons. I'm sure yours does too. During these times our communication and relationship can suffer. Marriage requires selflessness, maturity, and attention if growth is to happen. And sometimes, frankly, we're just not there. It's in those "sometimes we're not there" stages when any of us can look like dinner to a lurking lion! And at such weak moments—whether we're willing to admit it or not—we just might give in.

That's why it is so important for you and I to walk in the strength of the Lord rather than our own. We need to realize that our bodies are the "temple of the Holy Spirit" (1 Corinthians 6:19), and that He can give strength and self-control to every part of us—our hands, our eyes, our thoughts—most importantly sometimes, our feet.

If we will choose to honor and trust Him, even in our weakness, living in daily surrender to His will, He can help us through our most tempting times.

Even if they involve a cat woman.

⊕ Taking Aim

1. Think of a time where you were in a very tempting situation sexually and you knew it was wrong to give in. How did you handle it?

2. What did you learn—specifically—from how you handled the situation?

3. Read 1 Corinthians 6:18–20. What does the Bible say is so particularly dangerous about sexual sin?

4. Read Matthew 26:41. Write down the two things that Jesus says are so important in helping you resist the temptations of the flesh.

5

Bob

WHEN THINGS GET TOUGH

Fear not, for I have redeemed you; I have summoned you by name; you are mine. When you pass through the waters, I will be with you; and when you pass through the rivers, they will not sweep over you. When you walk through the fire, you will not be burned; the flames will not set you ablaze. For I am the Lord your God, the Holy One of Israel, your Savior. (Isaiah 43:1–3)

The Dark Continent. Its mystery and allure have long been a draw to hunters from across the world. And in my various journeys there, I have found it to be everything legend has said it would be.

My first experience in Africa was a mission trip, capped by a photo safari in Kenya. The beauty took my breath away, and the animals were spectacular. After that, I never cared about going to a zoo again.

A couple of years later, I was blessed beyond words to be asked to go to Uganda to speak, then to end the trip with a couple of days hunting in South Africa. The two days turned into five, and I was hooked! I had discovered a whole new arena for the hunting experience.

The animals there left me in awe. Their beauty, grace, agility, and cunning are beyond words. Spotting and tracking them is an experience I wish every hunter could savor. People ask me which is my favorite. I can't tell you. They're *all* my favorites!

But one animal that has stood out to me in a special way is the nyala—such a graceful animal, with beautiful markings. It is officially part of the antelope family but is bigger than the antelopes we see in America. Its markings blend in with the surroundings and literally make it "vanish" in the brush and landscape, right before one's eyes. The nyala is one of four curved horned Plains game throughout southern Africa, along with the bushbuck, kudu, and the giant eland.

But the nyala has a quality the other three are missing: it cries when it is injured, wounded, or dying. Tears actually role down its jawline and drop to the ground. Along its jawline are a series of white dots, and a white chevron forms an inverted "v" on the nose. The Africans say the dots are the "fingerprints of God," and the chevron represents "God's thumbs wiping away the tears."

Jump on a computer and do a search for "nyala." See an image firsthand, and you'll see what I mean.

What a picture—all the way from the heart of the Dark Continent—of God's care for us when we are hurting. I don't know about you, but this is a message I need to hear over and over again, because I repeatedly find myself hurting, wounded, or suffering as I travel the journey of life.

Take a moment and go back to the top of the page and read the verses for today. These words of Scripture—these words from God's very mouth and heart—have become so important to me

that I've memorized them. They have become "life verses" for me, serving as part of the bedrock assurance of God's work in my life.

Not just mine, actually, but others as well.

I don't know how many times along the traffic patterns of life I have shared these same, touching words with someone who needed them like I repeatedly do. The response from others has consistently been something along the line of, "I've never seen that before. I can't thank you enough for sharing those with me." These verses give us a needed perspective regarding our difficulties—how God knows us by name and knows exactly what we're going through. He will not leave us alone in the midst of it.

He has promised that in His Word.

How about you? Having any tough times recently? Not sure where to turn? Could it be that God seems inattentive, unresponsive, perhaps too late to be of any real help now? Have you questioned where He is when you need Him most? Maybe someone you care about is struggling with some of these very questions.

The answer is: He is right here where He has always been. He is present. And He knows where you are. He is there to help you through the pain, hurt, disappointment, anger, betrayal, or suffering. Regardless of how you feel, He will not leave you or forsake you. The God of all creation stands ready to wipe your tears away, even if they are only inside where no one else ever sees them.

Hundreds of years ago, the prophet Isaiah used idioms we still use today. Today it sounds more like, "I'm up to my neck!" "Things are just moving too fast!" "I know I'm going to get burned." But whether expressed in the language of Isaiah 43, or in the way we say it today, it still means the same: "I'm hurting and I need help, God!"

He assures us through those ancient words that He will be everything we need—and that ultimately, He alone will be our deliverer, regardless of what we are facing.

Now that is a *great* God. And the nyala is a great picture of the grace of God.

⊕ Taking Aim

1. What is a specific difficulty that you (or someone you care deeply about) is going through presently? Has the question honestly arisen, "Where is God, and why isn't He handling this?"

2. What meant the most to you as you reflected on today's Scripture?

3. How do you feel in being reminded that the God of all creation knows you *by name?* What about the promise that even in the midst of your trial, He will remain in charge and will see you through?

- - -

Lord, I'd never make it if You weren't here.

6

Bob

WISDOM
FOR THE JOURNEY

They did not receive the things promised; they only saw them and welcomed them from a distance. (Hebrews 11:13)

Well, it was August and I took the plunge. I picked up a good bow, some carbon arrows, and 100-grain practice field tips and broad tips for the hunt. With target in hand, I headed for some secluded land and began to hone my skills. And for good reason—I was headed to Colorado for elk!

After all, why start small?

Arriving at the north Colorado ranch, I quickly changed and headed to the field. My friend and guide, B. J., was an experienced hunter, far beyond his twenty-eight years. "Remember, Bob, *anything* you get with a bow is a trophy," he counseled. "This is your first hunt, so if you get a shot at *anything*, I'd take it."

I heard his advice, just as it was passing in one ear and out the other. I was there to bring home a 6x6, first hunt or not.

The predawn morning was crisp, the stars bright, and my

anticipation high. The trees were shimmering with hues of autumn gold. And the bulls were bugling. *Look out, world (and bulls)—here I come!* But nothing appeared at all during the whole first day and a half. What was wrong? Didn't they know I was here for a trophy?

It wasn't until 3:30 on the second day, as I sat in a ground blind, that the earth trembled with a bugle only seventy-five yards behind me. I almost came out of my skin! Peering through the brush, I could see the mass of this powerful bull, stomping and pacing—now *sixty* yards away.

Breathlessly hunching down, I waited for the moment when he would give me a shot. Time seemed to stand still. Then he whirled and stood broadside, a perfect target, but still about sixty yards distant. Too far away for a brand new archer. No shot.

Unperturbed, he snorted, looked my general direction, then strolled off over the ridge, taking my hopes along with him.

The following morning saw us up before dawn and positioned in timber adjacent to a large bed of willows, where we suspected some elk had been bedded over night. Sounding a bugle call, we received three answers in return. Hurrying through the timber, we made our way parallel to the willows and into the blind. The more we called, the closer he came.

My heart was playing calypso music. I just knew he would steer our way, I'd draw my bow, he'd step out, and—*zing!*—down he'd go.

As the bull nudged his cadre of cows into the sparse timber around me at forty yards, B. J. whispered, "You've got to decide . . . cow or bull?"

"I'll try for the bull," was my confident reply.

By now, at least five cows had moved their way across our visual path, coming in on the one side of the blind with the least cover. We could hardly breathe! Then I saw the dark brown mass of the bull's antlers appear on the edge of the timber. Drawing back, I labored not to make a sound. With the bow drawn, I waited for his fatal step.

And that's when the cows spooked. We'd been busted. And my heart was shattered.

Defeated and disgusted, I released my draw and slumped to the ground, muttering "What did I do wrong? What stupid mistake did I make? What does it take to succeed at a bow hunt?"

That's when B. J. stopped me in my tracks. "Bob, we worked two and a half hours this morning to pull those elk in. The weather was great. They responded like a storybook. We got to see the whole small herd up close and personal. You had a clear shot at the lead cow and could have had her easy. I'm telling you, many a man or woman can hunt elk for years and never experience what you've seen this morning. And remember, this is your first hunt.

"Remember, Bob," he continued, "there's more to the hunt than *getting a bull.* Everything leading up to that moment is 80–85% of the hunt. And you seemed to have missed it all because you were so focused on just *bringing something down.* If you're going to be like that, maybe you ought not to hunt. You'll miss too much, and savor too little."

With that, my young friend voiced the wisdom of a seventy-year-old veteran. Wisdom I needed to hear.

And not just for the hunt. For life in general.

Looking back, I fear I've too often focused on the ultimate accomplishment desired, and only succeeded at missing significant portions of the journey getting there. It can happen at home, at work, on trips, with relationships, and even on a hunt.

How about you?

 **Taking Aim**

1. Where in life are you missing the "journey" because you're too focused on the outcome?

2. What are some things you've missed enjoying by not relishing the in-between times?

- - -

Lord, what am I missing here?

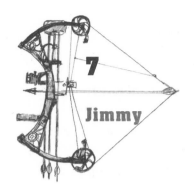

7

Jimmy

EJECTION SEAT TRAINING

Flee the evil desires of youth, and pursue righteousness, faith, love and peace, along with those who call on the Lord out of a pure heart. (2 Timothy 2:22)

Just outside of Le Castellet, France, is an airfield next to the Paul Ricard Circuit motorsport racetrack. Inside a hanger is an office belonging to MiGflug, an organization that purchases old fighter jets and refurbishes them. Cooler than that, civilians like myself can actually purchase flight time in one of these fighter jets with a pilot. And if you know me at all, you know it's been one of my lifelong dreams.

For whatever reason, I had fixated on an Albatross L39 fighter jet, the trainer for the Russian MiG. It's a fast, sleek, aerodynamic warbird with a forward and rearward cockpit for a pilot and copilot—a mean machine that regularly pulls six g's. And having witnessed my fixation on the L39 for several years, my amazing wife, Amanda, surprised me with a birthday present. We were off to Europe to spend a day with MiGflug at Le Castellet!

After meeting Stephanne, the retired French military pilot who at one time had been part of the French equivalent to the Blue Angels, I signed release forms and began my training. For the next two hours we covered topics such as how to handle a high g-force without a G-suit, the proper use of the barf bag, the importance of focusing on the horizon when doing loops and rolls and turns, how to steer the plane by stick. We also discussed our airspeed, our flight plan, and the use of the Go-pro cameras that would capture the action on video.

Most of our time, however, was spent covering only one specific topic: the ejection seat.

The L39 has an ejection seat for each pilot. And underneath or within the ejection seat are enough rockets that, should you be catapulted out of the canopy, you would initially experience twelve to twenty g's or more—definitely not survivable if it lasted any longer than it actually does.

Back injuries have been the major source of reported injuries related to ejections from aircraft, specifically compression fractures. Approximately 30 to 50 per cent of those who have ejected from aircraft have experienced some sort of fracture during the process. Arms and legs have even been torn off pilots who failed to tuck properly. Still others have ejected while the plane is upside down, thus shooting the pilot straight into the ground. It is scientifically proven that pilots who have experienced an ejection from a plane are so compressed by the experience, they can be up to a half-inch shorter afterward (which is still better than being dead)!

The whole idea, of course, is to get out fast in case of danger. And that is exactly what happens—*whoom!*—if you pull the red lever.

Here's how it works. The crew boss that fitted me into the back seat of the cockpit strapped me in with a four-point seat belt harness, then said, "Fold your arms across your chest and do not move until I tell you to." He then proceeded to pull a cotter pin from a red lever.

"Number one, hot!" he said as he pulled the pin. What that meant is that the ejection lever, if pulled, would immediately shoot me straight into the air.

I noticed that the pin he pulled had a triangular metal tag attached to it, displaying the word "Danger." This pin was attached to a small cable that ran to *another* red lever.

"Number *two*, hot!" the crew chief said as he pulled the second cotter pin—the plan B lever in case lever #1 failed.

By the end of the routine, the crew chief had pulled *five* cotter pins to *five* red levers or buttons, any of which should propel me out of the aircraft (or, if all else failed, blow the canopy off the plane so I could get out, being careful to dive really hard left or right, he told me, so the tail of the plane wouldn't slice me into two pieces).

A lot to remember. A lot to process.

Danger. Eject. Survival.

The crew chief gave me a thumbs-up and awaited my reply. I gave a thumbs-up in response, as did Stephanne the pilot. The canopy shut and eventually we were soaring.

Needless to say, I didn't touch any red levers or buttons! Had the situation called for it, however, and had Stephanne said through the microphone into my helmet these words, "Eject! Eject! Eject!" I would have immediately pulled the red lever. Better to take my chances ejecting out of a dangerous situation than to stay in it and crash and burn.

Life is the same way. You may find yourself in a crash-and-burn situation. It could be an affair or a pending affair. It could be an addiction. It could be a self-centered lifestyle that's spiraling out of control. It could be a business that just isn't going to make it. Or maybe you're stuck in the mud of unforgiveness. It could be any number of things.

While it may be tough to do, and while it may result in all kinds of negative implications, your only choice of survival may be to eject from the situation. In some cases, there is truly no other way out.

If so, tuck in, say a prayer, and grab the red lever. Do it now! And if the first attempt doesn't work, go to the next lever. If none of that works, then blow the canopy and dive out. It takes an incredible amount of courage, but you can do it.

Don't crash and burn. Eject! And live to fly another day.

 **Taking Aim**

1. Read the story of Joseph in Genesis 39. He was tempted to have sex with a beautiful woman who was the wife of his boss. Did he eject or stay in the situation?

2. Were there any negative implications to what Joseph did?

3. Continue reading the story of Joseph in Genesis 40. Were there any positive implications to Joseph's "ejection" from the situation?

4. From what or whom do you need to eject?

- - -

Lord, do I bail?

8

Bob

YOU JUST CAN'T HIDE STUPID

A happy heart makes the face cheerful, but heartache crushes the spirit. (Proverbs 15:13)

A cheerful heart is good medicine, but a crushed spirit dries up the bones. (Proverbs 17:22)

Have you ever done something stupid on a hunting or fishing trip? If so, you know by firsthand experience that you just can't hide it, no matter how much you'd like to.

I had been given the right to hunt on a beautiful piece of land owned by a developer friend. It was pristine, filled with rolling hills, a well worn ridge that ran along toward hilltops, marshy bottoms, plenty of oak and persimmon trees, and no hunting traffic!

Autumn had turned frosty in the morning, remaining cool-cold during the day. I had been out on the land, scouting to discover where the deer were moving, what their corridors were, where the bedding and feeding areas were, and where the transition paths lay just inside the wood lines. It was going to be a good season! I could feel it in my bones.

The signs had been plentiful. And some of them were big! I didn't have access to trail cams, but my eyes could take in all the indicators.

I had built a ground blind at a juncture where I saw three trails coming together, leading from the bedding area to a grazing field and stream running from the lake. This had all the signs of being a gathering place and watering hole. Before long, my hunch proved true—in spades! There he was! One of the largest ten-points I had ever seen. He was standing regally at the edge of the woods, right by the area I had staked out, as though overlooking his domain. His muscled shoulders gave the appearance of an experienced warrior. The tines on his horns glistened in the rays of sun, sparkling with remnants of the early morning frost.

Needless to say, I was exhilarated with anticipation.

Hang around here, big boy. I'm coming for you.

Two days later, on the morning of my planned execution, I hadn't slept more than a couple of hours. The excitement was boiling up inside me. I had showered and properly de-scented, arriving significantly before dawn in order to slip in and be in position before daylight. Everything was working according to plan.

I parked my F-150 a sufficient distance from where I would be hunting, not wanting the deer to spot it and be spooked. I had taped down the door switches on my truck so that opening the doors wouldn't automatically turn on the lights. Quietly, I slipped out of my cab and into my hunting jacket. I even held in the door handle so that in pushing it closed, it wouldn't make a sound.

Then all chaos erupted. Sliding my hand into my backpack to assure my truck keys were safely tucked away—ready to chauffeur me back a little later, my victory smile lighting up the rearview mirror—my finger evidently hit the alarm button on my truck remote fob. The horn started blaring. Headlights began flashing. I started panicking. And every deer within ten miles headed for cover!

It's in times like these that our true selves come to the surface, and we face a choice: to lose our temper, or to just . . . what're you going to do?

As a younger guy, I can *tell* you what I would have done. An experience like that would have likely ruined the whole day for me. And if anyone had been with me, my attitude would likely have ruined their day as well. My anger in such a situation probably stemmed from a fear that I wasn't quite adequate to my task.

But hopefully I've learned a little something from the "school of hard knocks" over the years. And as I sat on the ground, disappointed in myself, the thought crossed my mind how absolutely stupid I must look to the deer. I could see my circumstance as a great captured moment for a *Far Side* comic strip.

And I started laughing.

Choosing to laugh made all the difference.

If we are always ready to laugh at ourselves, we'll never run out of material! Most things that happen to us are just really not that serious, so if we can learn to laugh about it, we become able to take life in stride. And the people around us will join us in our laughter a lot more.

When you experience these kinds of "failures" in life—like my morning in the deer hunt—learn to share them with a smile rather than a frown, admitting you're still on a learning curve. As someone once shared with me about communicating with others, "Share your victories and successes and you'll build walls; share your struggles and challenges and you'll build bridges."

Do it with a smile and a laugh, and you'll build a Golden Gate Bridge of relationships!

 Taking Aim

1. Do you remember an instance when you messed up fishing or hunting and your primary response was anger?

2. How did you feel a day or so later? How did anyone else who was with you feel as they observed your response?

3. If you had it all to do over again, how do you wish you would have responded?

- - -

Lord, are You laughing too?

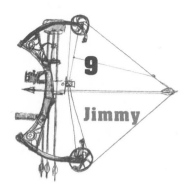

9

Jimmy

THE ADVENTURE
OF LIFE

*Whoever listens to me will live securely and be free from the
fear of danger. (Proverbs 1:33)*

I can no more avoid an adventure than a living person can avoid
the next breath. Adventure calls to my soul like a siren in the
fog of night, singing her compelling song. Adventure seems to
find me. And if not, I find *it*.

The battle I'm usually fighting is the dullness of life. I don't want
such dullness to exist, and where it does, I wage war against it. To
kill it. I want to *live*—whether I'm on the next hunt, at worship with
the church, on a date with my beautiful wife, cheering at a football
game, or spending time with my children. I want to squeeze out
every drop of life that God offers while I am traveling through this
world. I want to live a life that counts, to drink from the deep wells,
to run with gazelles, to fly with eagles, to hunt with lions, to love
like Jesus, to give like a martyr, to laugh life a pardoned prisoner.

I want adventure!

I remember well the day before I was to leave with my family and two cameramen to travel to the Amazon jungle in Ecuador. I would be producing a documentary on a Stone Age Indian tribe, an experience that included living, eating, and hunting with them for a few days. I was sitting at my desk reflecting on what was about to happen. I wrote these words in my journal that day:

> I leave in thirty-two hours. In a few days I will be hunting, eating, sleeping, and living with Mincaye and other Auca warriors of the Waodani tribe who speared to death Jim Elliot, Nate Saint, Ed McCully, Roger Youderian, and Peter Fleming in 1956 when they tried to take the gospel to this Stone Age tribe. I will travel by jet plane, bus, bush plane, dugout canoe, and by foot on jungle trails. I will be in peril of giant anaconda snakes, leopards, caimans, wild boar, poisonous frogs, Conga ants, and cannibals that shrink your head, not to mention diseases and all sorts of parasites. Adventure? Yes! I'm ready. And the best part is that my family is risking it all with me in order to help the tribe. That's what LIFE is all about.

Adventure is what makes a man or woman fully alive. When the element of danger is present—and oftentimes it is—that just adds to the euphoria I feel during the experience. Danger stirs my heart of hearts. It's not that I go out looking for it, but I'm not afraid of it—at least not when I'm in the wild of God's outdoors. I'm much more scared of cancer or car wrecks than I am of facing a bear at ten yards with only a bow in my hands, or a charging peccary on a jungle trail. The worst fear I have is receiving a phone call or a visit from a policeman informing me of tragic news regarding my wife or children. I hope that never happens, but I'm all too aware that it could.

I want to live, not hide in an office the rest of my life. I want to walk where no man has walked before. I want to face the impossible and at least give it a try. I'm not afraid of failing. Is that what drives me? I think it is simply living by the rhythm of God's heartbeat He has placed within me.

The Amazon trip turned out to be the adventure of a lifetime for my family and me. It forced me to look into the deep recesses of my heart and ask if I was really ready to face the ultimate challenge—to live the ultimate adventure, times ten!—possibly facing my own death in service to God in a very risky and dangerous place.

I can truly say I was ready. God had *made* me ready.

In fact, I think that trip helped me discover the true meaning of my existence on earth: *I exist to give everything* (whether I always want to give it or not). I was born with nothing more than my body and spirit; I will die with nothing more than my spirit alone. And since even my soul belongs to God, nothing is mine. All that passes through my hands on earth is simply that: "passing through."

I live to give. I give myself. I give my possessions. I give my heart. I give my love. I give my mind. And in so doing I relinquish control and ride the wind of adventure.

That's life in the fullest measure.

 **Taking Aim**

1. What is the greatest adventure in the wild you have ever experienced?

2. What did you learn from that adventure?

43

3. God promises in Isaiah 41:10, "Do not fear, for I am with you; do not be afraid, for I am your God. I will strengthen you; I will help you; I will hold on to you with My righteous right hand." What does this mean to you?

4. If you are going to experience fear in life, the best kind of fear is mentioned in Proverbs 1:7: "The fear of the Lord is the beginning of knowledge; fools despise wisdom and instruction." How do you "fear" the Lord?

- - -

Lord, I give You everything.

10

Bob

IT'S ALL IN THE TIMING

For my thoughts are not your thoughts, neither are your ways my ways," declares the Lord. (Isaiah 55:8)

When the time had fully come, God sent his Son. (Galatians 4:4)

When I've put a lot of thought and planning into something, and then it falls through, I'm not the happiest guy in the world. And that's exactly what happened last year.

I had wanted to go elk hunting at a place I'd heard about through a friend. He had gotten a great big bull there—a monster—and in hearing him describe it, I could already envision myself taking one just like it. (OK, maybe just a little bit bigger.)

So last year I planned to go myself. I had made the contacts, done the research, and even plunked down the deposit. Things were on GO!

That's when the shoe fell.

45

My wife was reviewing my travel schedule, including my work in Washington D.C., speaking across the country, family commitments, and the like. And I noticed a scowl creep across her face—which is never a good thing.

When I inquired what the problem was, her words hung in the air: "Do you realize how much you're going to be gone this coming year?"

A long, painful conversation ensued. Several, in fact. And from that I learned a key difference between males and females.

When someone asks a male if he's free at a certain time on a certain date, men turn their calendar to that page and see that it's either open or not. Women, on the other hand, not only look on that *one* calendar date, but also check the dates before and after to see what other demands surround it. Sounds smart—as most women are. And yet at the same time, it makes *absolutely no sense!* Either the date is open, or it's not!

Needless to say, all my explaining, reasoning, rationalizing— yes, even begging—was to no avail. My trip was postponed into the next year. And for days afterward, I'm sure I walked around as if I was attending a funeral wake.

Now, fast forward a year.

My son had been posted in his job in Germany for three years. During that time, he had given us our first grandchildren—twin boys. And we had done everything possible to see them at least a couple of times a year. But when I found out my son and his family were rotating back to the States, and that he would be here a few months before taking an assignment overseas again, I made him an offer he couldn't refuse: "What would you think about an elk hunt?" When he said, "That would be awesome," life cata- pulted upward.

The two-day drive to the hunt provided some of the most

enjoyable days I'd spent in a long time. We laughed, shared stories, and discussed significant stuff as well as nothing in particular, all at the same time. Among the main topics we talked about were being an effective dad and husband and a man whose life God can bless. Add to that the fact that the weather was great, and we had a real winner!

The first day of our hunt was crisp, chilly, and spectacularly clear. Within an hour of getting into the woods, we were surrounded by bulls bugling their heads off. So close, but no shots.

Later that afternoon, we sat on a high point overlooking a gorgeous green glade wrapped by tall timber. Idyllic. As we watched, straining our eyes to spot movement, suddenly my peripheral vision picked up on something. Slowly, majestically, a bull elk came in from our left, walking like a king to his waiting court.

As we watched him, our guide strained through his binoculars to evaluate the graceful giant. "He's a shooter, " I heard him whisper. "A 6x6."

Bryan raised his rifle slowly and rested his cheek on the comb. I heard him take a deep breath and let it out. Sighting through his scope, he took another deep breath, held it momentarily, then let out and squeezed the trigger.

The bull hunched up, lurched forward about twenty yards, and then wheeled around 180 degrees, staggering back in the direction from which he had come. By that time, Bryan had chambered another shell and squeezed the trigger. As I watched the giant fall, my hands shot into the air and a shout escaped my lips. I had seen my son get his first bull, and the smile that spread across his face etched itself in my memory bank for a lifetime.

And just think, I almost missed it. What if I had held to my plan rather than listen to my wife's concerns the previous year? What if I had bulled forward on my "wants" rather than listening to the small voice within me, cautioning about moving forward without reconsideration?

Everything God allows to come into our path is for a reason. His cautions are usually because He has something better in mind. Patience today can lead to the moment of a lifetime later. So the next time something seems to get in the way of *your plans*—maybe, just maybe, God has something better in store.

 Taking Aim

1. Think back to a time when something kept you from doing what you originally planned or desired, only to experience something better God had in store. Was it worth waiting?

2. What did you learn about the value of patience?

3. What did you learn about trusting God, even when it isn't easy?

- - -

Lord, my plans are Yours to change.

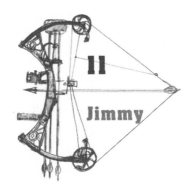

11

Jimmy

SUCCESS IN THE DETAILS

Be careful to do what the Lord your God has commanded you;
do not turn aside to the right or to the left. Walk in obedience
to all that the Lord your God has commanded you, so that you
may live and prosper and prolong your days in the land that you
will possess. (Deuteronomy 5:32–33)

As a professional hunter and outdoor television producer, my success is usually found in the details.

When I find an old whitetail buck I want to outsmart with my bow, I am fully aware it's going to be a chess match with that animal. He is one of the smartest creatures on earth, and I am going to have to dot every "i" and cross every "t" in order to get a shot.

The details start at home, where I am careful about scent on my clothes and my body. I wash my hunting gear in unscented detergent and store it in a large zip-lock bag with earth-scented wafers. I wear rubber boots rather than leather that breathes, and

I go into the buck's zone only when I am sure he will not see, smell, or hear me.

I am careful not to touch any trees or bushes with my hands, and I will not climb my ladder unless I'm wearing gloves. I walk like a deer when I reach the zone, careful to only sound like things the deer is used to hearing. I keep the wind in my face at all times. If the wind is wrong, I cancel my hunt for that day or go somewhere else. A smart old buck needs only one wrong scent or noise to send him two farms away.

I camo up to the hilt. Not one inch of my face, ears, or neck goes uncovered with the black, green, and brown face paint I use. I have a comfortable stand with my necessities at close reach, minimizing movement once I'm settled in. Sometimes I refuse to bring a stand into the area at all. On several occasions I have chosen not to do a single thing to prepare the area for my presence, knowing that I might only succeed in alerting the buck that something has been there. When hunting from the ground like that, I sneak in quietly and clear a spot in a honeysuckle thicket or a fallen tree, placing only a fold-out tripod chair in the makeshift blind, hoping to get off the shot before the buck even senses what's going on.

Paying attention to the details has put several trophy bucks on my wall. The same applies for my television production.

Most important, the same applies for life in general. If you don't believe that, consider Moses. He was the leader of the Israelites when they left Egypt and traveled toward Canaan. Because of their disobedience to God, the two million Israelites were punished by having to spend forty years in the desert of Sinai before going in to the Promised Land. While wandering there in the wilderness, they started complaining about the lack of food and water. So God sent them manna (bread) and quail. But they still griped—something about not having anything to wash down their meal with.

They were camped at Kadesh in the Desert of Zin at the time (Numbers 20:1–13), and God in His mercy told Moses to go to a particular rock and speak to it, that He would miraculously draw forth water from it. Moses already knew what God could do with inanimate objects. He had seen Him produce water from a rock before. He had even seen Him split the Red Sea and dry up the seabed so His people could cross from one side to the other on dry ground. But Moses was frustrated with the people he was leading. They were such whiners! And as he neared the rock, bristling with frustration, he took his staff and—instead of speaking to the rock—he struck the rock. *Whack!* Sure enough, out poured pure drinking water for the children of Israel.

Moses, however, was punished. *What? What did HE do wrong? He hadn't been the one doing all the moaning and complaining.* No, but he had struck the rock rather than speaking to it, as God had directed. And because of this, he was never allowed to set foot in the Promised Land during his lifetime.

One could say, "That sure does seem unfair. It's such a little thing!" But remember, success is in the details. Often it's the smallest things we do that make the biggest difference. This is true in hunting and fishing, in team sports and individual sports, in relationships, in business, in our health, and in our everyday life as well.

Be sure to dot every "i" and cross every "t."

It could change everything.

Taking Aim

1. Can you think of a time when the small details were what made the biggest difference for you in bagging a trophy?

2. When you make the decision to do something differently than what God has directed, how do you think God reacts to it?

3. You've been taught that God is gracious and forgiving, and He is. With that in mind, are there still any implications for what we might consider small disobediences?

4. Read Deuteronomy 3:23–26. Do you need to reconsider your answers to questions 2 and 3 above?

- - -

Lord, show me the small stuff.

12

Bob

DECISIONS DETERMINE DIRECTIONS

*How long will you waver between two opinions? If the Lord is
God, follow him; but if Baal is God, follow him? (1 Kings 18:21)*

Hunting and fishing, like all of life, are filled with points of
decision.

*Can you make the shot from this distance? Is this the animal
you want? Should you take the shot now or wait? Do you make the
difficult ascent to reach your animal, or will it be dark too soon?*

*Was that a hit on the line—do you need to set the hook—or was
it just a figment of your imagination? What's the right bait for the
fish in this area? What amount of weight do you put on the line so
the hook can sink down to the depth you desire?*

Decisions are the turning points of life. They make or break
life's experiences. And sometimes they make or break life itself.
That's why making the right ones—and avoiding the wrong

ones—is so very important. Some decisions will leave you with second chances, and others won't.

I can look back on my own hunting and fishing experiences, as I'm sure you can, and remember decisions that changed the outcome and made all the difference. That one decision may be why we can celebrate a trophy on the wall or a picture on the table . . . or why we only *wish* we could.

One of the unchangeable principles in life is this: *Decisions determine directions, and directions determine destinies.* In other words, key decisions in life determine the direction toward an outcome (good or bad), and those directions will inevitably lead to the outcome (destiny) itself.

And while this is true in your hunting and fishing adventures, it is also true regarding the most important decision of your life: *Who or what are you going to commit your life to follow?*

This is exactly what the prophet Elijah was challenging Israel to decide when he asked them the question at the top of this chapter. And in challenging Israel, he was challenging the men above all, for in God's economy they are the leaders of the home. Men will always have choices, but they cannot choose to avoid this: they are responsible for setting the example for others—their wives, their children, their families—of what is truly, primarily important in life.

So allow me to ask you if in your own spiritual journey, you have come to the place where you "know that you know" (where you're certain without even an ounce of doubt) that you have come into a personal relationship with Jesus Christ as both your Savior and Lord? Or, if you are totally honest, would you have to say, "I hope so," or "Maybe so," or even "I pray so"?

If any of those last remarks are what you'd honestly say, then you *don't* absolutely know. And God has told us that the Scriptures were written so you can "know" you have eternal life (1 John 5:13), beyond the shadow of a doubt.

But this requires a decision by every man or woman—a decision that no one else can make for him or her—not a parent, a sibling, a spouse, a pastor, his child or grandchild, or anyone else. It must be personal and total.

Have you done that?

By the way, being a follower of Christ is not primarily about going to church, or being on a membership roll, or having been baptized, or giving some money. Those are good things to do, but they're still only religious expressions. What I'm talking about is a living relationship where a man has surrendered his life to Christ, asking Christ to make him become all that he was created to be.

As we continue on in our journey together throughout this book, nothing is more important than deciding that you have settled this issue once and for all. So allow me to share with you four simple, straightforward points about God's desire for His relationship with you:

1. *God's design is for you to enjoy life and not merely endure it.* He said in the Bible that the reason He sent his Son was so you and I might not only have life but have it abundantly (John 10:10). And He wants you to experience this personally—by knowing Him, the way He knows you. "This is the way to have eternal life—by knowing you, the only true God, and Jesus Christ, the one you sent to earth (John 17:3). If this is true, why then have most people missed this reality?

2. *Our dilemma is our separation from God.* The Bible explains we each have a problem called "sin." To get a clear picture, look at it this way—sIn—with the capital "I" in the middle. The "I" is what sin is all about: *my* plans, *my* timing, *my* life, *my* control, *my* way. And this sin infects you and every single one of us, because

"all have sinned and fall short of the glory of God (Romans 3:23). "Your sins," the Bible says, "have caused a separation between you and your God" (Isaiah 59:2), whether you are living in active rebellion or passive indifference. Either way, sin is basically a declaration of your independence from God.

3. *God's deliverance is provided through Christ, His cross, and His resurrection.* The only answer to our sin is the Lord Jesus Christ. He died to pay the penalty for our sin. His death and resurrection bridged the gulf separating us from a loving God. As the Bible says, "God demonstrates His own love toward us, in that while we were yet sinners, Christ died for us" (Romans 5:8). Jesus is not merely one of many ways to God's forgiveness and eternal life. Nor is Jesus simply the *best* way to God. Jesus is the *only* way to a personal relationship with God. "There is salvation in no one else; for there is no other name under heaven that has been given among men, by which we must be saved" (Acts 4:12).

4. *Your decision makes all the difference either way.* God didn't make us robots but instead gave us a free will to choose. You are not forced to choose God. But you can. You can choose to be in a relationship with God through Jesus Christ by:

- Admitting your need ("Lord Jesus, I need you")
- Surrendering control of your life to God
- And receiving God's gift of a new life by faith

You can start by putting these actions into a prayer and just speaking to God from your heart, like this . . .

Lord Jesus, I realize I am a sinner. I am truly sorry for my sins, and I desire to turn in a new direction . . . in Your direction. Please forgive me. I know You died on the cross to pay for my sin. Right now I invite You into my heart. I surrender control of my life to You to be my Lord. I trust You now to be my Savior. Change my life and help me to live as You desire. Thank You for hearing—and answering—my prayer. Amen.

Now that is a *decision* that begins the change of *direction* in your life, and as you walk out your journey with God and others in faithfulness to His Word, you will find that such a decision not only determines direction, but also *destiny*!

⊕ Taking Aim

1. Whether you made this decision today or some time before, it is a first step. To truly follow and grow as a believer, get to know Him better each day by praying, thanking Him for His blessings, and asking for His daily guidance.

2. This devotional will help you get an ongoing, fresh perspective from God on living life His way by taking verses from the Bible and applying them to daily living. Keep it up!

3. Be sure you are involved in a church of like-minded and committed people who will help you become everything Christ created you to be.

- - -

Lord, I believe you.

(If you have made a decision to surrender your heart to God and your are starting a journey of great adventure with Him, please see "Your Harvest Record" on page 212 of this book.)

57

13

Bob

WHEN THE REAL WORK BEGINS

For it is by grace you have been saved, through faith—and this is not from your yourselves, it is the gift of God—not by works, so that no one can boast. For we are God's workmanship, created in Christ Jesus to do good works which God prepared in advance for us to do. (Ephesians 2:8–10)

Boom!

The rifle shot echoed over the ranch in the crisp, chilly, early morning Texas air.

I had been so nervous, my hands felt like the pre-tremors of a California earthquake. After all, this was my very first shot at a deer—not as a young, eager boy under his dad's careful eye, but as a grown man. My good friend Bud, owner of this ranch, had been after me for several months with an encouraging, "Just try it!"

So here I was. Trying it. My second day in the Texas hill country. And I had fallen in love with it the minute I had seen it. The hills and valleys. The babbling river, coursing through a rugged stone canyon. The sage and scrub brush, dotted throughout with pin oak. The well-beaten dirt roads, yielding access to the far-flung fingers of the property. Wrap it all together, and I loved it.

Bud had coached me well in deer-hunting technique, telling me to take a deep breath, then to let it out nice and slow. Take another as you sight through your scope. Then let it out slowly again. And just when you reach the end of that breath, squeeze—don't jerk—the trigger.

Ever since 0-dark-thirty, when Bud had dropped me off at the stand, I'd been working hard to execute his instructions exactly. And now, approximately two hours later, I had a buck on the ground! Not just any buck—my *first* buck! And I was pumped.

This nine-pointer wasn't the biggest on the ranch. I knew that. But to me, he was a giant. After all, the only hunting I'd done at that point in my life was kicking up quail as a young teen on my parent's farm in Illinois. I didn't even know there was any such thing as Pope and Young, or Boone and Crockett. All I knew now was: I had a deer! And my hunting jacket was about to rip open at the zipper from pride! (Is that even possible?)

After what seemed a three-day wait, Bud finally arrived with the truck, and we loaded up my trophy in the back. I bet I talked a mile a minute the whole way from there to the trailer where we were staying. Bud was probably wishing for a cork about that time. Then as soon as we pulled to a stop, I blurted out, "Do we take him to the taxidermist now?"

Bud chuckled good-naturedly, patted me on the shoulder, and said, "Bob, now is when the real work begins. Pulling the trigger is the easy part." With a smile, he grabbed a knife, handed it to me, and said, "Here. He's yours."

So began my first experience of field-dressing a deer.

Bud walked me through the anatomy of a deer with step-by-step guidance, occasionally giving me a helping hand. I felt like a certified surgeon. While it may not have been the most artistic field-dressing in the world, it did get the job done and I learned a lot. I was proud of having a hand (literally) in the dressing of my deer. And the smile on my face could have covered the state of Texas.

I've never forgotten that morning. Nor have I forgotten Bud's words—"Now is when the real work begins." How true that is of deer hunting, but also of following Christ.

I well remember the moment I decided to surrender my life to Christ, asking Him to become my Savior and Lord. What a rush! A highlight of my life's journey. I recall the sense of being washed clean on the inside (what the Bible refers to as *forgiveness)*. My relief and joy were immediate. I knew I had done something critically important. It would turn out to be the single most important decision of my life.

But that's when the real work started. God doesn't intend those who follow Him to simply "make a decision" and stamp their ticket to heaven. Our surrender to Christ is to be followed by a process of becoming everything He created us to become. It's a journey. And while it may have its ups and downs, the overall progress is meant to be upward. The goal: becoming more like Christ.

But it doesn't just happen. It requires work. Even though we don't (and actually can't) work our way to Christ in hopes of becoming His follower, and even though it's still His grace that keeps us moving forward and serving Him from then on, the work we put into our faith walk is a way of saying "thank you" for all He has done and is doing in our life. It's what proves the reality of this inner transformation.

Some key aspects of that work involve things like . . .

1. Getting active in a Bible-believing church to help you grow in your relationship with Christ.
2. Reading a part of God's Word every day and applying it to your life.
3. Hanging around Christ-followers who are further along the journey than you, people you can learn from as they show you what has helped them grow in faith.
4. Praying daily, taking time to thank God for loving you and calling you to Himself, confessing anything you've thought, done, or said that hasn't pleased Him, and asking for His guidance and provision for specific needs in your life.

Being a Christian does take time and effort. But you'll find the work is really worth it. I guarantee it.

 **Taking Aim**

1. How are you doing regarding the four items listed at this end of this devotional? What do you need to strengthen?

2. How would you describe your growth curve in your Christ relationship in the last year?

- - -

Lord, do Your work.

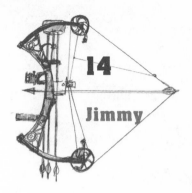

14

Jimmy

THE WAFFLE TREE

Consider it pure joy, my brothers and sisters, whenever you face trials of many kinds, because you know that the testing of your faith produces perseverance. Let perseverance finish its work so that you may be mature and complete, not lacking anything. (James 1:2–4)

I was turkey hunting on my friend Bill McDonald's Beaver Dam Creek farm one beautiful spring morning when I ran across what I quickly named the Waffle Tree.

I'm not sure what kind of tree it was. But at some point in its existence, whether from a lightning strike or high winds, this tree had experienced a traumatic split. Instead of having a single trunk anymore, it now had two—divided almost to the ground, all the way down to the base. One to the left, and one to the right, literally growing apart.

In addition, I noticed that decades earlier someone had used this tree as a living fence post, nailing four strands of barbed wire directly into each trunk. (Most people who spend any time in the outdoors have seen this common occurrence.) And as the years had gone by, the ongoing development of these two trunks had caused them to ingest the barbed wire deeper and deeper into their bark and flesh, as if slowly swallowing it. The rusty wire protruded as if coming from the middle of each separate trunk. (You've probably seen that sort of thing too.)

But what really drew my eye to this tree was something else that had occurred over the passing years. Many, many seasons of new growth had emerged from the trunk on the left, trailing horizontally along those four strands of barbed wire, while also growing up, down, and between, connecting to each other vertically. It gave the appearance of a waffle. The result was almost a new trunk formation with four arms reaching toward the right-hand trunk, seeking to draw the two together.

Although the tree had not fully succeeded yet in its slow mission of reuniting these radically altered trunks, it was making progress. And given enough time, the growth of that waffle core between them will grow so dense and heavy, those two trunks will one day stand as one again. Not perfect, but united. Not devoid of scars, but no longer divided either. Decades from now, a passerby might not immediately even detect that those two trunks had been so violently severed.

I snapped a picture of the tree on my phone and walked away thinking about the life analogies that can be learned from the Waffle Tree.

Life is not always easy. Sometimes life is traumatic. And what am I going to do with the trauma that comes my way? I can either give up, or I can grow through it. I can be bummed out or branch out. I can waste away or waffle up. The latter will take tenacity, willpower, and dedication. Most of all, it will take time.

But God promises to help me and never leave my side.

Through the good and the bad, He is willing to walk with me through life's hardships. He carries within Himself the power to make good things come out of bad situations, to turn broken people into healed people. Into whole people—actually the most whole people of all.

That's exactly what Paul was addressing in one of the greatest chapters in the Bible, Romans 8: "We know that in all things God works for the good of those who love him, who have been called according to his purpose" (Romans 8:28). God provides for me when I open up my life to receive what He offers.

The Bible talks about God's provision for the trees with this line from a song: "The trees of the Lord are well watered, the cedars of Lebanon that he planted" (Psalm 104:16). But if God provides for a tree, even a damaged one like the Waffle Tree, then He is surely going to provide for my needs, because I am created in His image! He is going to hurt when I hurt, and laugh when I laugh, because He cares for me. He is going to root for me when I face trials or temptations or tests. That's exactly what Peter stated in 2 Peter 2:9: "The Lord knows how to rescue the godly from trials and to hold the unrighteous for punishment on the day of judgment."

I know that high winds are going to blow from time to time. I realize that lightning will strike occasionally. I am not exempt from pain and hurt and tragedy. But when it comes, I want to grow around whatever gets nailed into me and onto me. I want to grow together, not apart, still joined with those I love and with whom I share community. I want to be a survivor. And some day in my future, I want people to look at me and see a stable old tree that has handled life well and is still bearing its best fruit.

 **Taking Aim**

1. Can you think of another illustration from nature that portrays how life's traumatic events can be overcome and how healing is possible?

2. Have you experienced trauma in your own life and been able to successfully heal and overcome it?

3. In what ways can God take something bad and make something good out of it?

4. If you want to read an amazing story about an overcomer, read the story of Job in the Old Testament. It is most likely the oldest literature found in the Bible, so even Abraham was probably familiar with it. It's a great read on a deer stand!

- - -

Lord, hold me together.

15

Bob

SOME THINGS ARE WORTH WAITING FOR

In his heart a man plans his course, but the Lord determines his steps. (Proverbs 16:9)

It took a long time for this fishing trip to become reality. Fifty-seven years, to be exact.

Hunting and fishing in the awesome beauty of the outdoors can serve as a suitable context for a lot of things: exercise, adventure, the thrill of victory, the agony of defeat. But perhaps one of the most important elements involve family relationships—even the ones that have taken a lot of time to come around.

Years ago near the western borders of Virginia, three little boys were born in stair-step fashion to a young couple. The wife and mother was a gentle, loving lady, appreciated and valued by all who knew her. The husband and father, on the other hand, was restless and a heavy drinker. Like most alcoholics, consistency and dependability were not his primary strengths. And when frustrated, those who were closest to him bore the brunt of his exasperation.

It was while the third of these boys was still in the womb that the mother was diagnosed with some significant physical difficulties, putting her own life in danger. Had the court rulings of *Roe vs. Wade* and *Doe vs. Bolton* legalizing abortion been in place then as they are today, the baby this woman was carrying might easily have been sacrificed. Yet carry the baby to term, this brave mother did.

But her trials didn't cease with the birth of her third son. Life took up about where it had left off early in her pregnancy. A drinking spouse, stressful scenes, short tempers—enough hardship and strain on a fatigued young mother until eleven months after the birth, she just couldn't keep going any more. Dying became easier than living. A brain aneurism ended her courageous journey, leaving a young father with three things he hadn't necessarily wanted or planned for: three boys under the age of four.

And life went from bad to worse.

For all of us.

I should know. I was the youngest.

Over the ensuing months, my brothers and I were swapped from hand to hand and place to place, with no location to really call home. Finally separated, we each went to new homes—the older two to one adopting couple, and me to another, after a series of additional handoffs. We grew up knowing nothing of each other's whereabouts.

Sixteen years passed. By then, all three of us had become young adults. I was preparing to graduate from high school, and the older two were already in college. Then on one surprising day, after all our time apart, we found ourselves sitting together, staring at each other, searching desperately for words, yet not knowing what to say.

Eighteen, nineteen, and twenty . . . and nothing to say.

Having been raised as an only child, I had watched television shows like *My Three Sons* and *Eight Is Enough*, wishing my family included some brothers or sisters. Now here they were, and I didn't know what to make of them.

Though we did get to be in each other's weddings, the bond that only seems to develop from growing up together in the same home was missing. While we kept in touch, it could never be the same. After all, "life happens"—college, families, careers, living in different places across the nation.

But in 2009, we *made* it happen. With a lot of planning, plenty of delays, some cancellations, and a strong dose of tenacity, we accomplished our first-ever vacation together as brothers. With the help of a friend's wonderful boat, we spent two days off the east coast of Florida, meshing our lives amid the salty sea air, the stench of bait, the rocking of the boat, and the threat of rolling storms. We laughed, told stories, caught up on each other's journeys—the victories and defeats, the dreams and disappointments, as well as our hopes and plans for the future. We also managed to catch our fair share of snapper, bonito, grunt fish, and king, topping it off with a swordfish that was well worth the wrestling match!

I'm sure you'd agree: there are few better ways to forge relationships than while hunting and fishing in the incredible, God-crafted outdoors. Defenses come down, laughs are plentiful, skills and patience are honed, victories are shared.

I will long remember those handful of days that saw separated brothers forged into a family. Despite the missed years, long delays, and the dearth of shared experiences between us, our lives truly did merge into a bond of brothers—fifty-seven years in the making.

It never ceases to amaze me—even when we find ourselves in circumstances beyond our control, in situations we did not create—God is still in charge. He is always working overtime to get us to a place where He can bless us, even if the journey seems difficult and confusing. That's because nothing is more important to God than relationships—our vertical one with Him first, and then our horizontal ones with each other.

If you have a relationship that's broken, damaged, or distant—perhaps with your kids or grandkids—don't wait fifty-seven years to see how much of it you can put back together. Do it now, regardless of their ages . . . or yours. It's a legacy you don't want to miss passing on.

⊕ Taking Aim

1. Who is someone you'd like to spend some focused time with, but haven't in a long time?

2. Why don't you plan a trip to the outdoors, call them, and invite them to go with you?

- - -

Lord, rebuild my broken places.

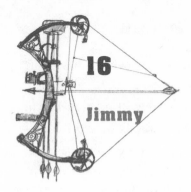

16

Jimmy

BUSH PILOTS

Do not worry about tomorrow, for tomorrow will worry about itself. Each day has enough trouble of its own. (Matthew 6:34)

I've found myself in some crazy situations with bush pilots.

In Alaska, for example, we were in a Cessna 206 coming in for a landing on top of a remote ridge. The "landing strip" (if you could call it that) was just long enough to work with if the pilot could stall the plane and then goose it to keep from nose-diving. With the "Stall Warning" alarm blaring in the cockpit, the pilot cowboyed the plane onto the rocky ridge, bouncing it on its balloon tires until we came to a rickety stop near the edge.

The wind was howling, so the pilot immediately began yelling, "Get your gear out quickly and clear the plane before it blows off the mountain!" Nice.

Three days later when the pilot returned to pick us up, we loaded our gear back onto the plane, along with 150 pounds of caribou meat tied under one wing and a caribou rack tied under the other. The bear-sized pilot, who looked like he hadn't seen a razor in five years, turned the plane into the wind. Reaching over to make sure my seatbelt was securely fastened, he turned on some bluegrass music in the headsets and poured gas to the little plane as we headed straight toward the cliff. We weren't even close to reaching the proper air speed before we went off the edge of the mountain, so naturally the plane began to plummet toward the ground. I just about crapped my pants.

As the earth drew closer and closer to our undercarriage, the little plane struggled to pick up enough air speed, finally getting some lift under the wings. I could feel the plane begin to level off. The g's were like a roller coaster on steroids.

Once the 206 hit the bottom of its descent and began to gain altitude, I actually breathed again. It was then that I realized I had been holding my feet up, trying with all my body English to help lift the plane as the tops of the trees were closing in. At that moment the pilot relaxed his grip, exhaled a deep breath, looked at me and said, "You ever read the book 'Wild at Heart'?"

Very funny.

On another occasion I was in a similar plane with jungle missionary Steve Saint and my daughter Christin. We were flying into the Amazon jungle in Ecuador, and the upper canopy of the trees seemed as if it was reaching out to touch the tires of our four-passenger plane. From the back seat I could see the "runway" approaching in our path. It was just wide enough for the plane to fit in, and it certainly didn't seem long enough to handle our flight speed. I could also see the back of the motorcycle helmet our Ecuadorean pilot Henry was wearing. I began to wonder why we didn't have helmets on as well!

Once again, the only way to get the plane on the ground safely was to almost stall it, thus reaching an air speed that was stoppable within the short distance to the end of the runway. Henry pulled it off, however, as if he was managing a routine daily task like riding a bicycle or eating breakfast. Meanwhile I was puckered so tight, my two posterior cheek buns could have fit in a coffee cup.

It was all worth it, though, when I looked left out of my window and caught my first glimpse of the Waodani Indians who had come to greet us, complete with face paint, Peccary-tooth necklaces, and arm-length tattoos on each arm shaped like a continuous W with dots in between.

It's moments like these when a person recognizes that the calculated risk of adventure is worth it. Life is too short to live in fear of what might happen, especially when more than 80% of the things a person worries about never happens anyway.

Worry is a joy killer. Worry stifles creativity. Worry robs experience. Worry can even cause you to work for more stuff because you think you don't have enough, or to be overprotective of what you do have because of fear you might lose it.

Jesus makes it clear, "Do not worry about what tomorrow" (Matthew 6:34). He also said, "Do not worry about your life, what you will eat or drink; or about your body, what you will wear. Is not life more important than food, and the body more important than clothes?" (Matthew 6:25). I think part of what he meant is to get out and live life to its fullest. Don't miss opportunities. Squeeze every drop out of every day.

A very important question to ask is this: "If I live to a ripe old age and am no longer able to get out and do things, will I look back and have regrets about anything I didn't do?" If your answer is yes, then quit worrying and get out there and do it—to the honor and glory of God.

After all, He is your pilot.

 **Taking Aim**

1. What things do you worry about the most?

2. Of all the things you've worried about in the past, how many have actually happened?

3. What does Jesus mean in Matthew 6:34 when he says, "Don't worry about tomorrow, for tomorrow will worry about itself"?

4. Read 1 Peter 5:7. How can this verse help you in your strategic plan to overcome worry?

- - -

Lord, what am I worrying for?

GIVING IT
ALL YOU'VE GOT

Whatever you do, work at it with all your heart. (Colossians 3:23)

Everybody needs heroes. And Chester is one of mine!
But Chester isn't a guy. Or a girl, for that matter. Chester belongs to Gary, lives in South Africa, and is a Jack Russell. That's a dog, if you're not familiar with the breed. They're smaller than a beagle and bigger than a Chihuahua, but with a heart bigger than Texas!

My first time out with Chester and Gary—my PH (Professional Hunter)—we were glassing from a high ridge, overlooking a luscious river valley. What a great place for game! The only problem was that none of it was within a reasonable stalking distance, and it was late afternoon. That meant the light would be fading soon, especially in the valley, as the high ridges where we were standing blocked the sun even before it fully disappeared in the West.

That's when we spotted them—two sizable nyalas. They were walking along the river's edge, deep in the valley, and had just seen each other. By instinct, they began to proudly stomp toward one another in full rut splendor. It seemed only a matter of time until their heads clashed together in a fight for full-on male dominance. So while they focused their attention on each other, we ran onto a game trail leading down the side of the mountain, hoping to get into position for a shot before all daylight was gone.

As we reached a point about two hundred yards from the biggest nyala, we whipped out the shooting sticks. I quickly acquired the target moving out from behind a tree and squeezed the trigger. The animal hunched up, obviously hit (what we would later discover to be high on the shoulder) and slowly moved away. As we scrambled to get another shot, I fired too quickly and shot just over its neck.

That's when Chester took off, running into the brush. We heard his bark as he tracked the wounded animal, and we immediately ran after him through the overgrowth, thorns, and rocks to get there before Chester was hurt.

Within moments, we heard his loud, pained "Yelp!" fearing the worst might have happened. Sure enough, in trying to corner the wounded animal, it had turned on Chester and gored him. As we ran, we prayed it was not in a major part of his body.

Yet we continued to hear his barking, sounding like it was heading for the river. Then it was coming from *across* the river, raising Cain! We realized the nyala was trying to cross the river, and if it did we would probably lose him. But wounded Chester had crossed the river, too, and was now moving up and down the opposite bank . . . barking, growling, and limping, turning the nyala back our way.

Struggling through the rock-strewn, thorn-infested banks, we finally broke through to the water, finding the animal turned and standing in the middle of the river. I quickly zeroed in, squeezing off the shot to bring this chase to an exciting, successful end.

Just then, as the nyala sank to a half-submerged position, Chester dove into the water and swam to the point where its head and massive horns still rose above the current. Dog-paddling in between the horns, he sat himself right on top of the animal's head, as if to say, "Look who came out on top after all, Big Boy!"

Now that's heart!

You've got to love it!

Not until we'd lugged the giant trophy to the shore in the darkness did we discover where Chester's injury was: his back left leg. Thankfully, the puncture had gone through the fleshy part of the leg, missing the large vessels and bones.

Later that night, after dragging the nyala to the truck through the timber and fence wire left tangled from the floods of previous months, Chester rode back with us to the lodge, curled on my jacket and awaiting a dose of soon-to-be-administered penicillin.

You would think such heroics would merit the rest of the week off. But no! The next day, in equally rugged terrain, Chester was out there hopping on three legs the entire time. And often, rather than trailing us, he was leading us! It was as if he were saying, "What's wrong with you wimps?! Suck it up and give it your all!"

That's what Paul said, too, in the Bible. He challenged us to do whatever we do "with all your heart." Then he added a qualifier, saying we should give it our all "as working for the Lord, not for men." In other words, serve the Lord with everything you've got. And even when things are tough, know that you're living your life "to the Lord," not merely to please, impress, or outsmart other people.

Chester reminded me that if *he* could give it all for the sake of a hunting trophy, how much more should I be willing and capable of giving everything *I've* got in serving and following Christ, who is worth so much more than a nyala hide!

How about you? Would you say you've got a "won't quit" heart like Chester's when it comes to your obedience and service to Jesus Christ? If not, why not? More important, what are you going to do today—this week—to make that happen?

⊕ Taking Aim

1. Think of the various areas of your life—marriage, family, work, church, community. Are you giving your absolute best to your responsibilities there?

2. If not, what is one thing you could change to raise the bar on your contribution?

3. If you're by chance thinking, "But you don't know my situation and what it would take," review today's devotion and think what both Chester and Gary were willing to do to get the job done. What does that say to you about stepping up to the challenge, even when it is not easy?

- - -

Lord, I'm not quitting.

18

Bob

I CAN DO ALL THINGS

I can do everything through him who gives me strength.
(Philippians 4:13)

Have you ever been tracking a wounded animal in haste, racing against the setting sun and deepening shadows, hoping against hope that you'll finish the chase before all hope is lost? I've surely been there, and so has most every hunter I know (if he or she is telling the truth).

One of the classic examples from my own experience involved the nyala hunt I just described in the last chapter. You remember my telling how we spotted it on a high cliff overlooking the river valley; how we raced down a steep, overgrown path in the gathering darkness; how Chester the dog was gored in the leg while chasing the wounded animal; and how he swam over and stood on its massive, bobbing head in the middle of the river. *Gotcha!*

What I didn't tell you was this: the hunt took place during South Africa's winter. And though bringing down a prize nyala was a grand accomplishment, we now had the task of pulling that enormous creature from a shivering, cold river before the nyala sank to the bottom, with the sun already hidden behind the canyon ridge.

Brrr!

Before I could move or think or process the situation, Gary (I noticed) was already stripping down to his underwear.

"What in the world are you doing?" I cried.

"I'm doing what has to be done. I'm going in for the nyala."

By the time he finished his sentence, he was already up to his waist in the cold current. "You come into the shallows," he said, shouting instructions, "and be ready to pull it to shore when I get it to you. Our time is limited, and we have to get this guy in as quickly as we can. We sure don't want jackals to start showing up. So get ready!"

By then, he was up to his chest in the freezing water, tugging on the dead animal. What an effort! Nothing stopped him. The job had to be done, and he was going to do it. In Gary's mind, this wasn't somebody else's job to do. He wasn't waiting for anybody to show up and take responsibility. He was stepping up to the plate, meeting the task—no matter how dark, no matter how cold, no matter how dangerous.

Struggling together, Gary and I lurched that enormous beast to the bank, falling to the ground in exhaustion just to catch our breath. Shivering in the night wind, Gary struggled to get back into his clothes.

Mission accomplished, right? Wrong!

While we had been laboring through our present challenges, our tracker Nevell had run back up the mountain to where the truck was, driven it down the steep, rutted road, and gotten as close to the river as possible. *Oh, right—we weren't finished yet.* Now we had to get the animal, with all its dead weight, into the vehicle.

Don't the challenges ever let up?

79

Looking back on that night, I've often thought how it's not what it takes to *move* a man that reveals his character, but what it takes to *stop* him. How often I have been tempted to let trials and challenge stop me. More times than I care to admit, I've asked myself, "Is this really worth it?" I've been ready to let someone else fight the battle.

When the challenges in your life are tough, do you put your shoulder to the plow and get the job done? Are you willing to do what it takes to step into the fray and move through the difficulty? Or do you hesitate, back off, and second-guess yourself?

If Gary could do what it took that night in the cold waters of South Africa, imagine what you can do through the power of Christ! After all, God has promised to make you equal to any task you may face. Nothing—did you hear that?—*nothing* is impossible for Him. He is everything you need for the challenge before you.

So don't just stand there—*dive in!*

 **Taking Aim**

1. Is there a challenge you are facing right now in which you need to ask God for special help? What is it? And what is the specific help you need?

2. Rather than avoid the challenge, what is one step you could take to step into the issue and address it, rather than letting it just keep on going?

- - -

Lord, You can do anything.

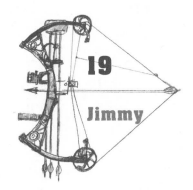

19

Jimmy

RACING WITH JOHN ANDRETTI

*I have fought the good fight, I have finished the race, I have
kept the faith. (2 Timothy 4:7)*

I recently had the opportunity through my friend Tom Anthony
and his staff at IMMI (Indiana Mills and Manufacturing, Inc., a
leading designer of advanced safety systems) to meet up with race
car driver John Andretti. John and I were chosen to be spokesper-
sons for IMMI's seat belt safety campaign. What better way for a
couple of guys to endorse seat belts than to put them to the test!

IMMI designed a new three-point safety harness and installed
prototypes in a Polaris Razor. They also built a dirt test track in
a wooded area north of Indianapolis, complete with moguls, a
rock climb, sharp curves, a mud pit, holes, logs, steep inclines,
and anything else they could think of to create an authentic test
for what outdoorsmen might encounter in a wilderness setting
while driving a UTV.

The day came for John and I to sign the death or injury waivers, strap on our helmets, and have some fun. He was driving (needless to say) while I buckled into the passenger seat. It wasn't long until I was white-knuckling as we slid around curves, throwing mud onto cameramen as they shot video and stills of the action. There were a couple of occasions when I thought we were going to be testing the roll cage on the Razor as well as the seatbelt harness. But somehow John managed to maintain control of the little souped-up UTV. I guess there's enough of his uncle Mario Andretti's blood pumping through his veins that he can pull off the impossible in anything with four wheels!

That is, until exactly one hour and thirty-one minutes into the test drive.

It was at that exact moment we went airborne over the moguls and slammed head-on into a tree that just happened to be in the way. The Go-Pro footage of our faces as we hit the tree and then looked at each other is hilarious. But the seat belts had done their job, and John and I walked away unscathed. (Can't say the same about the Razor . . . sorry, Tom!)

But it was actually the *other* part of my Andretti adventure that caused me the most anxiety.

John had invited us to come to his hometown of Charlotte, North Carolina, and meet him at the Charlotte Motor Speedway. The Mario Andretti Racing Experience is available on the track there, a school that people can go through and actually drive a race car around the track at high speed. John explained to me that I would get to ride with him in a two-seat Indy car, and then would be allowed to drive one by myself. *Holy smokes, Batman!* I couldn't sleep for three nights before the trip!

During my plane ride from Nashville to Charlotte, I wrote in my journal. Here is my entry from that morning:

Today I will come as close to death as a healthy man could possibly come. I will be an inexperienced driver who is driving an Indy race car at speeds of 160 mph around curves. The wall of the Charlotte Motor Speedway will be just to my right, and John Andretti will be on pit row cheering me on. There will be three other Indy cars on the track with me, and someone in the control tower will be giving me instructions in my headset that sometimes are hard to hear. I am told by those who have gone through the Mario Andretti Racing Experience that it is actually not fun while you are driving at top speeds, but rather the most frightful thing they have ever done. One miniscule mistake or one tire blowout, and chaos explodes in your face. The fun is when you pull up at the end and get out of the car, realizing that you survived, and comprehending what you have just done. A euphoric feeling washes over a person at that moment. God, please see me through to that moment!

I can see some spiritual analogies here.

In a sense this seems to parallel in a small way my adventure with God. It is a frightful thing to place myself into the hands of God . . . the One . . . the Creator . . . the Commander of the armies of heaven and the One who directs the Death Angel. Just seeing God's face would kill me instantly. Yet He has invited me to drive on His Eternal Life Speedway, and I have accepted. He is my Father, and I am His adopted son. And so I drive "pedal to the metal" through life, not having ever done it before. I buckle up, strap on a helmet, and keep both hands on the steering wheel. I listen to the directions of the One in the control tower. I stay alert and roll into each day with a prayer on my lips.

It's not always fun. Sometimes it seems like a little bit of hell on earth. But if I stay the course and finish the race, there is a crown of righteousness awaiting me. I will get out of the car, take off my earth suit, and experience joy like I have never known. That will be the greatest moment of adventure for me, when I see God's face and live forever!

By the way, I survived the amazing Indy car experience and can now say I've driven fourteen laps at 160 mph. I can also say that I've survived a crash with John Andretti, and even ridden in a car with him at 170 mph, close enough to the wall at Charlotte to reach out and touch it. These truly were some of the greatest moments of my life!

But the best is yet to come.

 **Taking Aim**

1. Paul wrote some very interesting words in Galatians 5:7: "You were running a good race. Who cut in on you to keep you from obeying the truth?" Wonder what he meant by that?

2. List some of the things in your own life that could be considered as "cutting in on you" as you drive on God's Eternal Life Speedway.

3. Did you crash? Or did you implement a maneuver to keep your speed steady and your race car stable?

4. Read and reflect on the following words found in Hebrews 12:1–2: "Therefore, since we are surrounded by such a great cloud of witnesses, let us throw off everything that hinders and the sin that so easily entangles. And let us run with perseverance the race marked out for us, fixing our eyes on Jesus, the pioneer and perfecter of faith."

- - -

Lord, I'm all in.

20

Bob

OUNCE OF PREVENTION

"If it pleases the king, may I have letters to the governors of Trans-Euphrates, so that they will provide me safe-conduct until I arrive in Judah? And may I have a letter to Asaph, keeper of the king's forest, so he will give me timber to make beams for the gates of the citadel by the temple, and for the city wall and for the residence I will occupy?" (Nehemiah 2:7–8)

When Nehemiah began making plans for returning to his homeland of Israel, set to lead the rebuilding project for the broken-down walls of Jerusalem, he needed to make sure he had what he needed and understood the requirements he would face once he got there.

Nearly a hundred years had elapsed since the people of Israel had returned from exile. And while the temple had been rebuilt, the fortifying walls around Jerusalem had not. Therefore, the city remained sparsely occupied due to the resulting lack of security within. And because the people were living outside the city, intermingling with myriads of foreigners and their pagan ways, the Jewish people were rapidly losing their unique identity.

That's when God called Nehemiah, a key confidant and trusted servant of King Artaxerxes of Persia, to return and lead the people of Israel to rebuild. But Nehemiah knew better than to launch out ill prepared or uninformed to face the task.

His preparations would prove to be invaluable. The walls of Jerusalem, which had lain in ruins for a century, would be rebuilt under Nehemiah's stellar leadership in just a matter of fifty-two days. In no small part due to his foresight and attention to detail, he would lead a seemingly impossible task and mobilize an army of people for the assignment at hand.

I have learned the same type of preparation is crucial for hunting and fishing trips, especially internationally. Traveling in America, pretty much all you need to do is be sure your ammo is in its original box, throw it in your gun case, check it with TSA at the airport, and be checked through to your destination.

Not so overseas. In South Africa, for example, although your ammo can usually make it into the country in the same bag with your clothing (if packed separate and apart from your firearm), things can change unexpectedly when you depart. Depending on the airline, the time of day, or even just the particular agent you're dealing with, you may well be required to put your ammo in a separate, small, hard case secured with a lock, to be treated as its own piece of luggage. If you don't have one, if you didn't bring one, you may just lose your ammo. So you need to throw in a small, lockable case before you leave. You may need it on your way back.

In addition, you'll want to be sure to make a copy of all of your credit cards (front and back), your passport ID page, driver's license, gun permits, TSA authentication for your guns, and U.S.

Customs declaration forms. You can carry them separately in a carry-on bag or a small USB jump drive. You can also have someone reliable back in the U.S. keep a backup copy for you. This way, if anything is lost or stolen, you'll have a much easier time defending your identity while answering questions in a culture not your own.

When it comes to your money and vital documents like a passport, a secure front pocket (as opposed to a back pocket)—or better yet, a concealed money belt or neck lanyard packet—will prove to be a wise strategy. There are few things worse than being in another part of the world only to find that your cash, travelers checks, and travel documentation are missing. A bit of preparation and study of the culture to which you are traveling can make all the difference!

Lastly, there are a number of places in the world where you can be adventuresome in the hunt, but not when venturing anywhere else without clearing it with your outfitter first. For several years, African cities with international airports have been relatively safe for travelers within the confines of the airport property. But if you range outside the safe harbor of the airport, things can get a little dicey, as far as your susceptibility to pickpocketing, muggings, and robberies. In places such as South Africa, the more rural areas have been safer for many years, but in recent times have increasingly become tenuous for those who are not native to the country or unaccompanied by a knowledgeable and equipped guide. You may feel all brave and secure with your "I can handle whatever may arise" attitude, but this presumption can quickly prove foolhardy.

Being properly prepared for any circumstances that may arise can make all the difference, both in hunting and in life. Nehemiah had it right. Better safe than sorry. And the results were success!

 **Taking Aim**

1. What steps do you need to begin taking today which will help ensure success in a key task that's facing you in the next several weeks?

2. Thinking in spiritual terms, what is one thing you need to do to prevent a possible misstep in your life for which you could be very sorry later if you don't avoid it?

3. Since Scripture advises us, "I have hidden your word in my heart that I might not sin against you, (Psalm 119:11), how are you doing in putting at least one verse of Scripture per week into your memory bank? If not, why not start this week?

- - -

Lord, prepare me.

THE EYES HAVE IT

The eye is the lamp of the body. If your eyes are good, your whole body will be full of light. But if your eyes are bad, your whole body will be full of darkness. (Matthew 6:22–23)

Like you, I've often wondered what gives a deer that sixth sense of visual radar that can lock onto a hunter's presence, based on no apparent reason or slip-up on our part. But after doing a little research, I've discovered a lot more about these amazing creatures we seek to outsmart with our silence, strategy, and stamina.

Here are some good things to know . . . or remember.

Deer have a very wide field of vision. A band running across their retina allows them to take in a very broad scope of perspective at any one time. When we humans look at a distant object, we see a relatively narrow snapshot of the subject we're viewing, but the deer sees almost the entire horizon at once. This is why it pays to be above the deer in a stand if at all possible.

But not only can they detect range, of course, they detect movement. The vast number of rods in their retinas allows them to notice even the slightest flex or shuffle from a hunter who hasn't learned to be completely still and quiet.

And yet this same acuity of the deer's can also play to the hunter's advantage. Attaching a tuft of toilet paper to the rear of your decoy, for example, letting it flutter there in the gentle breeze, can snag a buck's attention and draw him in closer to investigate, especially during the rut. A human probably wouldn't even see it; a deer will spot it almost every time.

And if you've ever wondered why they don't see blaze orange, this is only due to the fact that they don't see longer light wavelengths, as humans do. But wear even a hint of any other color that contrasts with the woods and its camouflaging surroundings, and we know we're just asking to be busted.

What about their amazing ability to navigate in the dark? The makeup of a deer's visual senses give them approximately fifty times more capacity to process available light than we can. So while the darkness closing in around us hinders our vision as humans, it actually helps the deer see much more clearly and distinctly, allowing it to travel, feed, and congregate with other deer all night long.

This tells us that working our way through the woods before dawn not only doesn't hide us from the deer; it may end up increasing our chances of spooking them. We're usually better off waiting until there's just enough light for us to see to get to our stand, which also helps us get there more quietly.

Without question, eyes play a very important role when it comes to hunting—both the deer's eyes as well as our own. Understanding our own capacities and limitations of visual acuity, as well as those of the game we are pursuing, is critically important. Add to that the importance of great optics in being able to spot and stay on-game, and we're talking about the essentials of successful hunting.

But obviously, our eyes are important in every aspect of daily living. Jesus said the eye is the light of the soul. Through these key portals of the human body, we allow both good and bad into our inner being. So a big part of cultivating a healthy internal life requires being extremely careful about what we allow to enter through our eyes and what we protect them from seeing.

Lustful images, for example. The character Job in the Old Testament said, "I made a covenant with my eyes not to look lustfully at a girl" (Job 31:1). Keeping our eyes pure is no accident. It comes from a courageous, intentional decision about what we will (and will not) let ourselves look at.

Study after study has shown that many men struggle with online porn, some studies indicating that more than five out of every ten men who *attend church* are hooked on it. We understand the body chemistry that makes this an issue. We know men are typically driven by the visual. And so we're warned by God in Scripture to keep ourselves from letting our eyes lead us into sin and toward a seared conscience.

But it's not just men. Current research findings show that women, too, are being lured toward pornography in increasing numbers. Why? Because younger women have been raised in a shifting culture in which visual media is not only more pervasive than ever, but also more effective in shaping what is deemed appropriate and acceptable. Add to this the fact that many women, desiring romance and excitement in their marriage, have so completely sidelined their husband in focusing on the needs of their children, they no longer have the relationship they once enjoyed with their man. When they want it back, he's not always as available (not to mention the fact that he's usually put other things ahead of his marriage as well). Clearly, this is a tank trap of disaster, too easily filled with romance novels, escapist television, online chat rooms, and (more and more) pornography created especially for the female perspective.

The eyes are a gift from our Creator, both for the hunter and the hunted. But they are also a trust. God gives us the gift of sight and then trusts us to be careful with what we let pass through their gateway. This is how we protect our soul from being damaged by allowing the wrong stuff in.

 **Taking Aim**

1. In what ways are you allowing your eyes to wander in directions they shouldn't?

2. What are two steps you can take to ensure you don't end up looking at things that take you further away from Christ rather than closer to Him?

3. On the positive side, are you regularly getting your eyes into God's Word? If not, why not start this week with a commitment to read from your Bible at least five out of seven days, each week for the next three weeks? (Research indicates we can start a consistent, new habit over a period of approximately twenty-one days.)

- - -

Lord, lead me to guard these two eyes.

Bob

THE ULTIMATE GUIDE

"Come, follow me," Jesus said, "and I will make you fishers of men." (Mark 1:17)

Boarding the plane to Colorado, off to hunt bull elk with three great friends in some of God's most magnificent creation, I just *knew* I would get a big boy! The rut was expected to start that week. The guide had started hearing bugles. I was carrying a new Mathews bow. This time was going to be my destiny with a monster.

But don't we know, things don't always work out the way we planned or expected. Even when great experiences happen on the front end, it doesn't always mean our hopes will be fulfilled according to our dreams on the back end.

But I'm getting ahead of myself . . .

When we arrived on the beautiful eight-thousand-acre ranch, surrounded by another seventy thousand acres of land accessible to our guide, our hopes were off the charts. We just knew our treasure was out there and within range. Having been assigned our guides, we discussed the areas where we would begin five days of what we knew would be an awesome hunt. Stephen and I (my friend from Dallas) would be led by Trey.

It didn't take long to see that Trey was an accomplished guide. He had been doing this kind of work since his teen years and was now in his late twenties. His prowess in the dark timber and hill country was so second-nature, it would have been evident to a blind man. His cow calls sounded like the real deal, and I was convinced the bulls would come running with caution thrown to the wind.

But that was before the week settled in with a full moon, a rut that didn't start as expected, and temperatures warmer than normal by some twelve to fifteen degrees. The bulls just weren't ready to respond to calls. Spot and stalks became "spot and spook." We did everything possible—stealth, quiet, and scent reduction, bolstered all the while by Trey's amazing skills. But nothing was working. Nothing.

Not until the fourth day did a bull finally hold up, eighty yards away. One of them later came within forty-five yards amid heavy, tangled brush, but would never step into the shooting lane. That evening, we spied a magnificent five-by-five with huge G3s, chasing him down mountains and through ravines until dark (which meant we had to go back *up* them in the dark)!

Finally we reached the last afternoon of the hunt. Every grasp at the brass ring had come up empty. This was make-or-break time. We found ourselves sitting with Trey on a rocky ridge scoping the heavily wooded ravines below. Nothing was stirring—only storm clouds that looked to be steaming our way, likely preparing to drench us on top of everything else. Talk about a washout!

You've certainly experienced that feeling—the disappointment of realizing, after all your hopes and preparation, that your hunt is likely to be a bust. It wasn't just us. None of the hunters at the lodge had gotten off a single shot all week at anything. But still, we were mighty dejected as we watched Trey futilely glassing the ridges and ravines, trying to help us make something special out of this trip, even at the last.

Did he ever.

Lowering his binocs and turning toward us, Trey suddenly said, "Hey, I've listened to you guys and the others talk a lot this week about 'following Christ' and 'accepting Him,' but what exactly do you mean?"

I felt like I had been hit by a two-by-four. Could it be that bagging an elk was not really the purpose of this trip for me? While I had dreamed of a big six-by-six trophy on the wall, could it be that God was at work calling up a *trophy of grace* instead?

We put our optics down, laid aside the bows, unloaded the packs from our backs, and focused instead on Trey's penetrating question. I could tell that Stephen was praying for the situation big time, as he allowed me to take the lead in answering Trey's probing inquiry. Step by step, point by point, we covered the gospel with the same thoroughness and commitment with which we had strived all week to approach a big bull.

To our thrill, Trey was locked on. Never once did he look away scanning for elk. Even the brewing storm did not distract his focus. He was locked down with the same intent concentration I had observed in him throughout our whole time in Colorado.

After about an hour of discussion, I asked, "Does this make sense to you?" Trey nodded his head in the affirmative.

I asked, "Would you like to nail down that commitment right here? Would you surrender to Christ in your life right now with us?" Again, he indicated "yes!"

I could have floated off the mountain.

When I led us in a prayer of surrender together, that very skilled and talented young man looked at us with moist eyes, stood up, and placed his arms around our shoulders. "You'll never know what this hunt has meant to me," he said. "I needed you guys."

We had gone out looking for elk, but God had given us something far greater. Not only did we have a new friend and guide for whose skills we had the ultimate respect and appreciation, we now had a fellow brother in Christ—all from a hunt we thought was going to end as a bust!

Keep in mind: "In his heart a man plans his course, but the Lord determines his steps." (Proverbs 16:9). I am glad my Divine Guide had everything in control. He always does.

Next time you go out to hunt or fish, keep your eyes open. It could be that God has more in store than you imagined too!

⊕ Taking Aim

1. Are there two or three people in your network of relationships that, you're fairly sure, do not know Jesus Christ as their personal Lord and Savior? What are their names?

2. Would you be willing to pray that God would begin to use *you* to build a bridge to their life, over which Christ may walk into their heart?

- - -

Lord, keep my eyes open.

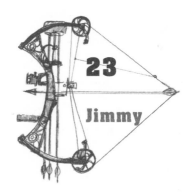

POCKETS
OF WILDERNESS

Come with me by yourselves to a quiet place and get some rest.
(Mark 6:31)

During certain periods of the year, I live in an editing cave. When those seasons are upon me, I spend even my off-days and holidays there—working. And when I do come out of the cave, it is only to eat, sleep, shower, or go to church. These are tough periods, but they're necessary.

You've heard the old saying, "You gotta do what you gotta do." I'm certainly not exempt from that statement.

But if I could get a break from the workload during these periods, I know what I'd do: *I'd go to Alaska.* There I could breathe in the wildness of that untamed region—the last great frontier. I could reseed the terrain of my heart. I could refresh my mind and clear the clutter. I could lay prone on the soft moss of the tundra and take a long overdue nap, awakening to a refreshed body. I could drink from a snowmelt stream cascading its way down the mountain. I could pick a hatful of blueberries . . .

Whoa—I just woke up drooling with my head lying on the keyboard here in my cave. The letter "R" is covering my entire computer screen—5,789 of them, to be exact. (I can't believe I counted them.) *Oh, how I need to get out of this cave!* If only I could go to Alaska.

Do you ever feel that way?

Here's what I've discovered during my lifetime, and I occasionally need reminders about my discovery. There are "pockets of wilderness" much closer to me than Alaska. It might be a friend's farm, a ten-acre tract of woods behind your house, a creek or river, a public hunting area preserved by your state, or a narrow strip of Corps of Engineers land between private property and the waterline of a Corps lake. I'm sure there's something out there within driving range, some place you can go to hang on to your outdoorsman's sanity.

Sure, you'll have to close your eyes when you come to the scars left by mankind. It won't be as pristine as the wilds of a Great Northern paradise. But with your eyes tightly shut, just imagine for a moment that you are standing on the Alaskan Peninsula. There is no one around you for 250 miles. It's just you and God and His beautiful creation. Oh, and watch out for that bear slipping up behind you!

I've learned that if I work too hard for too long, I reach the law of diminishing returns. That's when I need to get out of the cave and head to a pocket of wilderness. I may go there to hunt or fish. I may go there to hike or sleep. I may just go there to stump sit. (That's what I do when I'm facing a big decision and need to have some undistracted time alone to pray and think about the decision.) It's not Alaska, but it *is* refreshing.

During these short little outings, my main purpose is to rest my soul, which is a very biblical concept. Mark 6:30–32 reveals a story about rest:

> The apostles gathered around Jesus and reported to him all they had done and taught. Then, because so many people were coming and going that they did not even have a chance to eat, he said to them, "Come with me by yourselves to a quiet place and get some rest." So they went away by themselves in a boat to a solitary place.

I love this story, because I am far too often the victim of *overstimulation, overcommitment,* and *overload.* At times I need to quit doing and simply enjoy being. Sometimes I need silence. I need stillness. Yet quiet can be so deafening. Stillness can provoke such fidgeting in my bones! I'm not used to these two expert doctors of the soul. It is not my nature to be still and quiet. (That's what I have convinced my mind, at least.) But actually, I am slowly inching toward the realization that these *are* my nature, for God is in me, and God is the "gentle whisper" in the cave (1 Kings 19:12–13).

During much of my year, I will have to settle for occasional short treks to the pockets of wilderness, those nearby getaway places that still cling to their existence in small dots here and there. And that's OK. What's *not* OK is when I stop making these short pilgrimages.

I never want to get so busy that I can no longer discern the voice of God, who speaks to my heart in silence.

 **Taking Aim**

1. On a scale of 1 (worst) to 10 (best), how are you doing balancing your work time and your quiet time?

1—2—3—4—5—6—7—8—9—10

2. What happens to you when you become overstimulated, overcommitted, and overloaded?

3. What are some things you do that help you find silent solitude and private time with yourself and God?

4. React to the following statement: "The task of any leader is to help people concentrate on the real but often hidden event of God's active presence in their lives. Therefore, the question that must guide all activity is not how to keep people busy, but how to keep them from being so busy that they can no longer discern the voice of God who speaks to the heart in silence."

- - -

Lord, speak to me.

HURRY UP AND WAIT

The Lord is good to those whose hope is in him, to the one who seeks him; it is good to wait quietly for the salvation of the Lord. (Lamentations 3:25–26)

'm the kind of guy who, when he prays for patience, says, "Lord, give it to me now." I don't like sitting around. This is proven by the fact that Delta Airlines just informed me I will be moving from a Platinum Flyer to a Diamond Flyer. (What it *really* says is that I've been in a plane way too much!)

But I've always been a person of action. I love being on the go. Sometimes I say to my wife, Cheryl, "Let's go take a drive." When she asks where we're headed, I usually respond, "I don't know yet. I'm just ready to go somewhere."

Perhaps like me, however, you've discovered that a lot of life (like a lot of hunting and fishing) is comprised of "hurry up and wait." That's just the way it is. How often I have spent hours, sometimes days in the outdoors, waiting . . . and waiting . . . and waiting.

Don't get me wrong. I relish the experience of being outside and soaking in the majesty of God's creation, whether deep in the woods calling turkey, climbing the mountains after elk, slipping through a draw, lurking in a deer stand, fishing for bass in freshwater or for deep-sea varieties. But truth be told, I have spent many, many hours at these tasks—like you—simply waiting.

In fact, I just returned from Kentucky hunting deer with a great friend. And what did I spend my time doing? Waiting! For three days! And never saw a single deer! (Do you ever wonder how those guys on TV—like my pal Jimmy—make it look so easy? And how every ten minutes, a deer seems to come walking by them?!)

Ironically, however, God says that waiting is a critical part of life. There are evidently certain qualities of character that He only (or at least primarily) develops within our lives by causing us to sit through life's holding patterns.

Several key things God says we should keep in mind while waiting . . .

Wait alertly. God is always up to something, even when He has us in a holding pattern. He is most often preparing us for something that's coming in the future. So waiting is not a time for resignedly folding our hands and simply enduring. Instead, step proactively into your waiting periods. I've found two questions very helpful to ask when life has me trapped in a waiting zone: 1) "Is God trying to teach me something during this time?" and 2) "Is He trying to change something specific in me during this time?"

Wait expectantly. God says in Psalm 130:5–6 that we are to wait for God's eventual action with more confidence and expectancy than that which assures us the sun will come up tomorrow. "More than watchmen wait for the morning," the verse says.

That's a reference to biblical times when sentries were posted through the night to protect all those they watched over. Though the approach of morning to those watchmen may have seemed long overdue and delayed as they waited in the slow-moving darkness, they could always know—like *we* always know—that morning was sure to come. That's how confident we can be that God will move in the right way, at the right time, with the right answer.

Wait quietly and patiently. Have you ever read in the Old Testament how God liberated Israel from captivity in Egypt, how they were disobedient during forty years of wandering in the wilderness, and how they finally made their entrance into the Promised Land? When they came to the walled city of Jericho, God gave them an interesting directive. They were to circle the city one time daily for six days. On the seventh day, they were to circle it seven times. Then finally, at God's command, they were to shout. He promised the walls would come tumbling down. But have you noticed *how* they were to march around the city (Joshua 6:10)? *Absolutely silent!* Not a word was to be spoken. Why? Because God had undergone too much experience with them already. Every time things hadn't gone exactly like Israel thought it should, or whenever God didn't act in the time frame they expected, they always did the same thing—*complain!* So God told them to keep their lips zipped as they marched around Jericho because, given a chance, he knew they would have degenerated into bellyaching.

Sound familiar? It sure does to me.

But God clearly reminds us that the quieter we can be while we wait for life's answers, the less crow we'll have to eat—and when hunting, the more animals we'll see!

When I find myself waiting, I try to remember the motto of the U.S. Army Corps of Engineers: "The difficult we do immediately;

the impossible takes a little longer." I'm not sure about the army engineers, but I've seen God do the impossible over and over again. So if you are waiting for something right now, remember that nothing is impossible with God. Though you may be bored, antsy, or disappointed in the moment, remember that He can change your disappointments into His appointments.

Be sure you are waiting effectively.

 **Taking Aim**

1. Why is waiting such a difficult part of life? Are you waiting for something right now?

2. Do you find yourself striving with God's sovereignty in this waiting period? How are you responding?

3. If you had to counsel someone who felt trapped in a holding pattern of life, what would you say to them? Could you apply that same advice to your own situation?

- - -

Lord, take all the time You know I need.

25

Bob

A MATTER OF TRUST

Trust in the Lord with all your heart and lean not on your own understanding; in all your ways acknowledge him, and he will make your paths straight. (Proverbs 3:5–6)

I have fallen in love with Africa as a place for hunting. Never in my wildest dreams did I think I would have the opportunity to go there. I figured the closest I would come would be sitting in front on my TV, wearing my camo, watching others do it, and wishing I could be there. (OK, so I'm kidding about the camo!)

But in 2010, I found myself back in the Dark Continent with several friends. We hit the ground in East London, South Africa, with half of us heading northeast and the other half northwest.

Aaron hadn't hunted much, but he proved to be a quick learner, readily listening to our guides' (Phillip and Henny's) suggestions. This proved to be wise, enabling him to bring down a gorgeous kudu the second day. Many experienced hunters find it difficult to get a great one in several trips, let alone right out of the chute!

105

You can bet he was hungry for more.

Aaron and several of us had regularly noticed some impressive gemsbok (otherwise called oryx) on a far ridge. There were two good bulls, but they were so far away, none of us gave serious thought to getting a shot. Besides, the terrain was very rugged and steep between us and them. On our last evening there, however, Aaron couldn't take his eyes off that far ridge.

Henny, knowing that look, addressed Aaron with a question. "Would you like one of those on your wall?" With drool rolling down his chin in desire, Aaron nodded his head. "You know it."

"Are you willing to trust me?" asked Henny.

"I trust *you*, but I could never reach *that* with a shot," responded Aaron. "That's got to be at least 500 yards!"

"555 to be exact," Phillip chimed in. "But if you'll trust Henny and me, we can help you get him."

Eager, Aaron asked what he needed to do, and the guide posed a crazy question: "Can you picture the size of a shoe box in your mind?"

"Sure, but what—"

"I'll show you," Henny butted in. Telling Aaron to look through the scope, he instructed him to move the crosshairs three shoe boxes ahead of the animal's nose, and then raise it the height of what would be about six shoe boxes above that point.

"You've got to be kidding," cried Aaron. "I can't believe that will work!"

"Trust me," assured Henny confidently, "and you'll have a Gemsbok on your wall. Don't . . . and you won't."

Shaking his head in disbelief, Aaron raised the scope to his eye, settled his cheek on the stock, breathed deeply and calmed his nerves. *Three shoe boxes out. Six shoe boxes up.* Then a gentle squeeze on the trigger.

The crack of the rifle reverberated off the surrounding mountains. And nothing seemed to happen. With our eyes glued on the far ridge, we just knew he had missed. After all, the whole thing did sound a bit too crazy to work.

Then suddenly, the bigger of the bulls crumpled, collapsed, and began to roll down the mountain's steep incline. We all just stood there with our mouths hanging open.

The guide smiled confidently, gave a congratulatory nod, and said, "See, I told you. It's all about trust."

I'll never forget that moment—or how much it taught me about my relationship with God. He has promised to guide our steps and show us how to succeed in life if we will only . . . trust Him.

"I will instruct you and teach you in the way you should go" (Psalm 32:8). "In his heart a man plans his course, but the Lord orders his steps" (Proverbs 16:9).

And even when it doesn't make sense to us, He assures us that He knows what He's doing and will bring us to the point of successfully accomplishing what He has called us to do. After all, He will never guide us where He doesn't provide for us.

So how are you doing in your trust level?

 **Taking Aim**

1. What keeps you from taking God at His word and acting on His instructions regardless of whether you understand or have doubt?

2. When was the last time you hesitated to act on God's Word and it cost you?

3. What will it take for you to obey what He says, regardless of how you feel or think?

4. Are you convinced He can do what He says He will do?

- - -

Lord, I trust You.

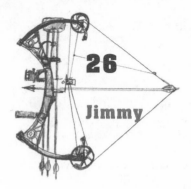

26

Jimmy

BE CONTENT WITH WHAT YOU HAVE

Keep your lives free from the love of money and be content with what you have. (Hebrews 13:5)

I climbed onto my lock-on tree stand this morning and reached for my hoist rope to haul up my backpack. My lightweight gloves were somewhat slick, and the small rope holding my backpack began cutting into my hands and then slipping down, causing rope burn. The backpack was so heavy, I began to wonder if I was going to be able to lift it twenty feet! Finally, after using some leverage with my boot, I managed to get it to the floor of my stand.

During my next two hours of hunting, I began to question why my backpack was so heavy. So I began rummaging through it. Here's a list of the items I found:

- Flashlight for tracking
- Headlamp with green light
- Wind tester
- Water bottle
- Food

- Grunt call
- Doe bleat can
- Contented doe call
- Cushion
- Scent elimination spray
- Deer attractant spray
- Archery release
- Camo paint
- Screw-in bow holder
- Range finder with ARC
- Binoculars
- C and D batteries for trail camera
- Memory stick for trail camera
- AA batteries for flashlight
- Cell phone
- GPS
- Chewing gum
- Knife
- Allen wrench tool
- Scent wafers
- Extra broadhead blades
- Scrape kit
- Folding trim saw
- Rain suit
- Bible
- Journal
- Pen
- Orange tracking tape
- Toilet paper
- Coffee thermos
- Chapstick
- Scent-free field wipes
- Reading glasses
- Anvil (not really, it just felt like it)

Upon completion of my backpack inventory, I sat on my stand and just laughed. How has it come to this? Do I really need forty-five pounds of gear to go hunting for a half-day, fifteen minutes from my house? I'm not saying it's wrong to be prepared and packed for every potential scenario, or to make the hunt as comfortable and productive as possible, but where do I draw the line?

Maybe about twenty-five pounds ago.

I think back to what hunting was like in my younger years, when I didn't have two nickels to rub together. I wore my dad's hand-me-down military fatigues. I used a bow that was purchased at a garage sale. I sharpened an assortment of used broadheads given to me by friends. And I created my own cover scent by placing a cedar bough in a zip-lock bag and beating it with a hammer to produce cedar juice, then soaking a small piece of cloth in it that I tied to my boot.

I learned to tell time by the sun's position and how to navigate the woods by the environment. Sometimes I got lost, but I always found my way back to the truck eventually. I didn't have a fancy, metal stand, so I built my own ladder stand out of scrap lumber, or just climbed a tree and sat on a limb. As far as a cell phone and all those other snazzy gadgets, they hadn't even been invented yet to clutter up my backpack.

Shoot, I didn't even *own* a backpack!

I don't see how anyone living in the twentieth century or earlier was able to kill a deer without all the stuff we're now told we "have to have!"

As I continued to reflect on these things while sitting in my deer stand, I thought of the time I spent with the Waodani Indian tribe in the Amazon jungle. These people are literally some of the poorest people on earth in terms of possessions. They make whatever they need from the resources they can find, cut, dig, or capture from the jungle.

The incredible Dayumae, for example—the same woman who taught Elisabeth Elliot how to speak the tribal language—helped my wife, Amanda, make two water jars. They shaped each jar out of clay and then baked them in a fire, hardening them.

The legendary Mincaye, who speared to death Jim Elliot and missionary pilot Nate Saint, carved a perfect spear out of peach palm wood and decorated it with toucan feathers.

When we went on a hunt with blowguns (also made by tribesmen), the great hunter Omena found a giant worm that was as big as a baseball bat, which got him to thinking. One of his buddies used some vines and palm leaves to weave together an ideal case to carry it (much like our gun cases), and they later caught two large Amazonian catfish with their new monster bait.

Pau, the tribe's best craftsman, seeing some cocoa beans high on a tree, looked around until he found a long vine. Winding it in circles and tying it off at the end—the same way you or I might put away a water hose—he planted both feet into the bottom of the circle, put both arms around the tree, and within twenty seconds, he had shimmied forty feet high. I stared up in amazement at what he was doing—until cocoa beans the size of tennis balls began raining down from the treetop and thudding all around me.

When he had collected all the beans he wanted, he zipped down the tree faster than he had gone up it, then stepped off his handmade climbing vine and left it on the forest floor. No more need for it. But now came the dilemma of how to carry this large supply of good-sized cocoa beans back to the dugout canoe, two miles away. (Surely you don't think by now he wasn't up to that challenge.) He sat down for about twenty minutes with various leaves and vines and constructed a perfect backpack, complete with a flap, clasp, and shoulder strap. Incredible! He deposited the beans into his new satchel, and off he went, smiling contentedly.

I could go on like this for pages and pages. This Stone Age tribe has learned the secret of being content with what they have. They don't hoard. You won't find their huts cluttered with a bunch of stuff. What you *will* find is an exquisite hammock hanging there, one that took them thirty days to make out of jungle vines. If they need to move—even if they need to flee a sudden attack—they've created a quick release on each end of their hammocks so they can grab them in a hurry and take them on to the next place.

These people are simple, yet profound. Poor, yet rich. They

have needs—like all of us do—but they have learned to satisfy their needs from what they have around them. And what they don't have, they don't worry about—and don't have to worry about losing. *They are content.* I guess that's why they're always laughing and happy.

I'd actually say they are the richest people I've ever met.

 **Taking Aim**

1. When Paul said, "Be content with what you have," what do you think he meant?

2. Do an inventory of your own hunting backpack. Make a list of the necessities and a list of the luxuries that you find in there, the things you carry with you on the hunt.

3. Now look at your life in general. Make a list of the necessities and a list of the luxuries that you live with on a daily basis.

4. Based on what you discovered, what changes do you need to make (if any) to live a more contented life—like the Waodani tribe? (Be realistic. You don't live in a jungle.)

- - -

Lord, You've already given me more than enough.

KNOW YOUR LIMITS

Then he [David] took his staff in his hand, chose five smooth stones from the stream, put them in the pouch of his shepherd's bag and, with his sling in his hand, approached the Philistine [Goliath]. . . . The Philistine cursed David by his gods. "Come here," he said, "and I'll give your flesh to the birds of the air and the beasts of the field." (1 Samuel 17:40, 43–44)

avid must have been sweating as he approached this giant of a man, the Philistine enemy Goliath. For days, the behemoth had taunted the fearful nation of Israel, challenging them to send a champion to fight man-to-man in a "winner take all" contest.

While King Saul should rightly have been God's man to step forth and lead his people, he was leading instead from the rear. At the very time he should have been on point, he was cowering in his tent. His increasing faithlessness had eroded his once revered leadership, turning a formerly valiant icon into a faltering, empty suit of armor.

When you're weak—like Saul—you assume everyone else is

just like you. Letting things slip here and there. Undisciplined. Avoiding facing up to reality. Not being honest with yourself. You can see it in how Saul attempted to transfer his own inadequacy onto David, trying to force him to wear the king's armor, warning him how big the challenge was, assuming he wasn't equal to the task.

David, on the other hand, had spent his years faithfully and quietly tending the flocks of his father. Out in those lonely fields, he had practiced his sling shots over and over again. He knew exactly what he could take out and at what distance. He knew success was never as easy as "practice makes perfect," but rather a case of "*perfect practice* makes perfect." As a result, he could nail a target at multiple distances—especially one as big as a giant, like the one who was now angrily standing in his way and defying David's God.

But just in case, he picked up five stones . . . not one. After all, even the best of shots can miss now and again. And even if he was dead on, further study reveals that Goliath had four brothers! (Now *that* is covering all the bases!)

A man needs to know his limits. This is especially true when it comes to shooting, whether by shotgun, rifle, or bow. Hunters must know what they can hit at what distance, and what they can't, long before they stride into the field.

According to Hoyt Archery, for instance, you might be interested to know . . .

- The average range at which a bow hunter hits mule deer is 35–40 yards
- This is twice the distance for the average whitetail shot
- Fifty percent of record-book elk are taken beyond 40 yards

The wise hunter needs to be sure he can draw and hit these distances in his sleep. The well prepared and experienced bow hunter will always work to get the closest shot possible to improve accuracy, of course, but he will repeatedly practice shots of up to seventy-plus yards . . . just in case. The time to try them is not in the field when you're suddenly faced with a shot requiring distances beyond your comfort zone.

That's why I try to shoot a few arrows every week. One of the bow hunters I respect most has said, "Start every day by stepping out your door on your way to the car and, if possible, shoot just one arrow. After all, when it really comes to taking a shot in the field, that's exactly what you will have—one shot. So practice that way regularly."

Great advice if you have a place to do it. That means no mulligan, like in golf. Just learn to make every shot count. Develop a reproducible pattern. Make each movement count.

The same is true in our spiritual and family lives. So let's take a look at these focal points:

- If you want your kids to want to spend time with you when they're grown, be sure you are spending time with them while they're growing up.
- If you want your spouse to be responsive to you, make sure you are responding to what's important to her, not just what's important to you.
- If you want to make wise biblical decisions when challenges come, be sure you're getting into God's Word regularly now—and getting God's Word into *you*.
- If you want a vibrant relationship with your spouse when the kids are grown and gone, be building that relationship now.

- If you want your kids to have great marriages and strong families when they grow up, make sure they see you and your spouse being strong and affectionate now.

David, because he knew his limits, took the appropriate steps and brought down a giant who had stopped everyone else in their tracks. How different history would have been if David had not spent the time honing his skills, testing his range, and knowing his limits. Having done all of that, no giant could stand in his way. The same can be true of you.

 **Taking Aim**

1. Where do you feel you're hitting up against a "limit" in your life that needs some attention in order to strengthen it?

2. What discipline in your spiritual life do you need to strengthen by repetition, realizing it won't get better without practicing it regularly? When do you plan to start the repetition?

3. What are the two primary lessons that impact your life in the story of David facing down Goliath? Who or what is your Goliath?

- - -

Lord, help me stay in practice.

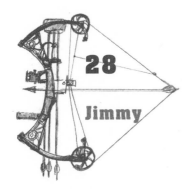

28

Jimmy

BUFFALO AND
SCHOOL SHOOTINGS

Who hopes for what he already has? But if we hope for what we do not yet have, we wait for it patiently. (Romans 8:24–25)

Country singer Craig Morgan was decked out in chaps, cowboy boots, spurs, Stetson, bandana, and cowboy shirt. As I climbed out of the teepee where we were lodging during our week on the old Santa Fe Trail in New Mexico, I noticed him standing on the lip of the canyon sipping coffee from a tin cup. He was looking at something far off in the valley below. He had likely spotted more buffalo—our prey for this particular hunting adventure.

Then I saw it myself. A cloud of dust kicking up, churned by something moving very fast, leaving a jet-like vapor trail in its wake.

Was it a . . . yeah, it was a truck. Which surprised me. Then scared me. Since we were filming an 1800s-era hunt with entirely traditional weapons, all the ranch hands and curious locals had been kindly asked to stay away from that area of the ranch unless it was a real emergency.

So that's what this must be—an emergency. Someone must have died, and word was being sent to us.

My, how I had underestimated the news.

The truck belonged to the long-legged, slow-talking rancher, who stepped out with a grim look on his face, tipped his hat, and said, "Boys, I have some bad news." The date was September 11, 2001. Camp ended abruptly for all of us that day.

Fast-forward eleven years. The date is December 14, 2012, and I am sitting in my office in front of the fireplace writing this very chapter. My plan was to work up the story of the terrorist attack on the World Trade Center and the Pentagon, trying to address the age-old question: "Why do bad things happen to good people?"

So I started by writing about cowboy Craig standing on the lip of a canyon looking down at something. You saw that. Then I got to the part where the rancher was stepping out of his truck to deliver the bad news. You saw that too.

That's when my Facebook page started dinging almost every second. (I should have turned the volume down on my computer.) I wanted to ignore it, but after so many hits, I was curious enough to click over and see what was happening.

And I couldn't believe my eyes!

One of the deadliest school shootings in U.S. history had just taken place in an elementary school in Connecticut. Twenty innocent children and six adults were dead because of one deranged young man. It made my heart sick to read the stories and watch the TV news.

Stunned, I stopped writing the chapter I was working on. I did, however, write something on my Facebook page. People everywhere were trying to make sense of this tragedy, and some of the things being written seemed to hurt more than they helped. I assigned myself the task of trying to put the right perspective on the tragedy in just a few words. Here's what I posted:

First, my prayers and thoughts to all who are affected by the terrible shooting that took place today. God never intended this kind of tragedy. He did not cause it, man did.

When God created the world He placed mankind in the Garden in Eden. Everything was perfect. That was God's original intent—the NATURAL ORDER OF THINGS. Then mankind listened to Satan's temptation and gave in to it, disobeying the one rule they had been given, eating the fruit in the middle of the Garden from the Tree of Knowledge of Good and Evil. Since the Tree of Life was also in the garden, God chose to expel them from the Garden lest they eat of that fruit as well and compound problems even more. It was an act of grace on His part.

Because mankind made the choice to rebel, sin came into the world. The natural order of things became the UNNATURAL ORDER OF THINGS. Death, storms, chaos, and evil became a reality, as well as the cause-and-effect pattern that is related to those things. God in His foreknowledge knew this would happen, so in His love and wisdom He developed a plan to offer a rescue to mankind: God coming to earth as a human to suffer and die for the very ones He created. Through this remarkable act of love, He offers mankind a way back "to the Garden" some day in the future. It is called "Heaven," and it will be perfection restored—the NATURAL ORDER OF THINGS once again.

The problem that you and I face is that we live in between the bookends of the Garden and Heaven. We live within the UNNATURAL ORDER OF THINGS. That's why bad things happen to good people, and good things happen to bad people. In the midst of it all, God occasionally reveals a miracle (not a supernatural event, but rather a glimpse of the natural—the way is was intended to be and someday will be). He does this to remind us of His original intent and His future plans for those who love Him and follow Him. Until that day, we just have to hang on to our hope of what is to come for all who choose to accept God's beautiful gift of grace. And we have to remain faithful even on days like this when we have a hard time wrapping our brains around why such tragedy occurs.

When I finally got back to that chapter I was writing about the terrorist attack on 9/11, I decided I didn't need to go any further into the details or statistics about that terrible day. Rather, I wrote the chapter as you are now reading it. The same purpose is served. Tragedy will always be with us. We are lulled to sleep by periods of peace and tranquility, only to be awakened by the next massacre or tragic event. It has been this way ever since mankind took that first bite in the garden.

That's why we need to "throw off everything that hinders and the sin that so easily entangles. And let us run with perseverance the race marked out for us, fixing our eyes on Jesus, the pioneer and perfecter of our faith. For the joy set before him he endured the cross, scorning its shame, and sat down at the right hand of the throne of God. Consider him who endured such opposition from sinners, so that you will not grow weary and lose heart" (Hebrews 12:1–3).

He's always here. And so there's always hope.

 **Taking Aim**

1. What is your reaction to the idea that we live in the era of the "Unnatural Order of Things"?

2. How can you hang on to your hope when things go really bad on earth?

3. God promises new heavens and a new earth in Isaiah 65:17–25. Various interpretations have been offered about the meaning of this passage. Read it in the context of the entire chapter and determine what you think about it.

4. The Israelite nation had disobeyed God so blatantly that He sent them into captivity. God promised to bring a remnant of faithful Israelites back to the Promised Land, including the city of Jerusalem, and to rebuild (which happened through Nehemiah). He was giving them hope. In what way does this serve as an analogy for what God promises to you in the afterlife?

- - -

Lord, give me hope.

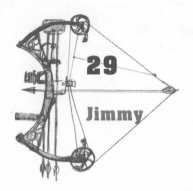

29

Jimmy

A LOST DAY

I do not understand what I do. For what I want to do I do not do,
but what I hate I do. (Romans 7:15)

ournal Entry—Day 2 (make that 3) of my New Zealand Trip:
The old saying that the mind can only take as much as the seat
can endure is definitely a truism. Trust me, I know. I've learned it
the hard way! I'm in the final hour of the flight from Nashville, Ten-
nessee, to Auckland, New Zealand. Seventeen hours in a plane seat,
all for the sake of hunting a red stag with my bow. And the curious
thing is that in crossing the international dateline, my Wednes-
day this week has completely disappeared. I departed on Tuesday,
April 17, and I am about to land on Thursday, April 19. Based on
the hours that ticked away in betwen, Wednesday, April 18, never
existed in my life.

Weird.

Or maybe a man's greatest wish. Have you ever wished that
one of the days of your life could be completely erased as if it
never happened?

1. The day you lost your job.
2. The afternoon you heard that someone you love deeply was hurt or killed in a tragic accident.
3. The morning when the doctor spoke the word "cancer" to you.
4. That day you found out about the affair—or worse, started one of your own.
5. That time when your rage overcame your rationality and left indelible scars on your child's heart.

The list is actually much longer. Isn't it.

We talked about this in the last chapter, but most things that happen to us are part of living between two bookends: perfection in the Garden before the fall of mankind, and the perfection still to come when Jesus returns to restore all things to their original intent. We live today in the era of *imperfection*—within the *unnatural* order of things. That's why bad things happen to good people and vice-versa. That's why we struggle with sin.

That's why we'd like to go back and erase certain days from our past.

But that doesn't mean there's no eraser available to us at all. God's love for us is so strong and His grace so powerful, He can clear the history on your sin—even the one that's been nagging at your conscience for years and years and years. The Bible says He can take them as far away from us as "the east is from the west" (Psalm 103:12). In other words, in God's eyes *it never happened.*

It's disappeared.

And you don't need to cross the dateline, because the cross pre-dates it all.

What sins from your past consistently distract your mind and keep you from living in a confident state of spirituality? Right now, at this very moment, I want you to consider truly accepting God's grace related to those sins and ask Him to erase the guilt you may still be feeling. Reclaim those lost days!

 **Taking Aim**

1. Find a blank piece of paper and a pen and make sure you are in a private area where no one can see what you are doing.

2. Write on that sheet of paper every sin that you can remember committing. (Be as specific as you want, or use generic categories like lust, adultery, cheating, lying, gossip, drunkenness, etc.).

3. Now draw a cross on the paper, above all the sins you've written down.

4. The power of Christ's blood accessed through the cross is strong enough to cover all of yours sins. As a symbol of this power to wipe away all of your sins and help you experience a new start, burn your paper until it is completely gone.

- - -

Lord, help me start over.

IT'S ALL ABOUT THE BASICS

*Be strong and very courageous. Be careful to obey all the law.
. . . Do not turn from it to the right or to the left, that you may
be successful wherever you go. . . . Be careful to do everything written in it. Then you will be prosperous and successful.
(Joshua 1:7–8)*

Where does the average guy or gal's mind go when they think
of a hunting trip or fishing expedition? The trophy, right?
Without question, our thoughts tend to jump to the outcome and
not dwell much on the process. After all, the process never makes
it to the wall or the picture gallery or even to the stories following
the event. We never hear someone say, "Hey, let me tell you about
the preparation I did to go on the hunt!" Or, "Wow, what a rush
it was to get everything ready and spend time making sure I had
exactly what I needed to succeed!"

No sir, we run straight to the result: "You've got to see the picture of this trophy." "Drop by the house and let me show you what I've got on the wall." "I'd love to tell you about the catch of a lifetime." "I never thought I'd take an animal like this one."

Truth be told, however, good outcomes only occur in proportion to the proper preparation invested on the front end. The proper equipment is essential. Making sure everything is in excellent working order is critical. Having backup equipment and planned redundancy in case something malfunctions is the better part of wisdom. Checking equipment and plans—and then checking them again—is as vital as squeezing off the shot or having the right bait.

This kind of work isn't exciting, exhilarating, enjoyable, or enticing. It takes discipline, dedication, and determination. It doesn't just happen; it must be intentional. But without question, it is essential!

I recently took a group to South Africa to hunt with my friend Glen Olivier of Mamlambo Safaris. I was looking forward to sharing an amazing experience with good friends in an awesome part of the world. But getting them there was a *lot* of work. Booking flights for everyone, making sure they'd secured their updated passports, assuring everyone had received their inoculations, helping them acquire proper paperwork for the safe transition of their firearms, arranging all of the ground transportation and lodging, checking that everyone had packed the right clothing— all of this had to occur before we ever set foot on South African soil or even sat down in the plane to get there.

But wait a minute—I thought hunting trips were supposed to be fun . . . exciting . . . beyond description!

That's true. They are. But they only get that way because of the basics that have been done on the front end to ensure success on the back end.

As you innately know, the same holds true in any sport. To be a great defensive player in baseball requires hours of fielding grounders and pop-ups. Hitting three-pointers requires tireless practice from behind the three point arc. Developing a consistent short game in golf doesn't just happen; it necessitates repeated practice from all angles of the green. Hitting quail, pheasant, dove, or chuckers well isn't just a natural gift, but rather the result of learning how to quickly acquire the target and continue to swing through when you pull the trigger. Getting good at anything takes lots of practice.

It's the same in our life with Christ. The success and exhilaration of success come only as a result of handling the basics—the things which nobody is likely to see or compliment, and yet the groundwork that makes spiritual growth happen and flourish. These things seem elementary, routine, almost nominal, insignificant. (See some of the questions in "Taking Aim" to see a little of what I'm talking about.) But in order to walk with Christ and experience all the freedom and adventure of the Christian life, nothing substitutes for doing the fundamentals with faithfulness, sincerity, and devotion.

So how are you doing in the basics? That's what God meant when He told Joshua to make sure he was regularly studying God's Word, treating it as life's "owner's manual" for effective living. Unswerving obedience to God's instructions would require not wavering to the right or the left, but staying focused on doing exactly what was required. It wouldn't be easy. Success never is. But like Joshua, we can get there by keeping ourselves principled and prepared, which takes no small measure of everyday strength and courage. "Be strong and courageous," the Lord said, because following God isn't for wimps!

If it was true of a warrior and "man's man" like Joshua, it is true of you and me as well. Take aim at the basics, and get ready for the best days of your life.

 ## Taking Aim

1. Are you having a "quiet time" in which you read the Scripture for your own growth, learning, and worship at least five of seven days each week?

2. Are you praying daily for guidance in all of life, not just when you find yourself between a rock and a hard place?

3. When you do pray, do you spend as much time thanking God for His blessings as you do asking Him for His actions on your behalf?

4. Have you shared your faith with anyone this year who wasn't yet a Christian, in hopes they might discover Christ? If so, what happened? If not, why not pray for the opportunity to do so before the year is up?

- - -

Lord, keep me basic.

Bob

THE COST
OF THE CLIMB

Endure hardship with us like a good soldier of Christ Jesus. . . . If anyone competes as an athlete, he does not receive the victor's crown unless he competes according to the rules. The hardworking farmer should be the first to receive a share of the crops.
(2 Timothy 2:3, 5–6)

As I looked up the sheer, steep side of the mountain . . . and as I heard my guide coaxing me to climb as fast as possible . . . and as the rock shifted and slid down the mountain with each step . . . I had only one thought: "If I live long enough to get a shot at this animal, and if I ever get to mount it on my wall, I think I'll put my guide's head right next to it for taking me up the side of this mountain!"

The day was crisp and crystal clear. My guide was only twenty-two but hunted as though he'd shown up with forty-two years of experience. We had spotted two gemsbok from the base of this mountain, after which he had casually said, "We can make it up there easy."

"Easy for *you* to say," I thought as I looked up the steep mountain.

The next thing I knew, we were driving up the mountain as far as we could (enduring a flat tire in the process), before taking to foot as we clawed our way up from one outcropping to another. Before long, I was panting like a dog in the August sun.

At twenty-two, mountains are minor challenges. But after middle age, they become major obstacles and overwhelming hurdles. Call it tenacity or maybe just stubborn pride, but I wasn't about to give up!

"Just a little bit further," my guide coached. *Didn't he say that three ridges back?!*

I pushed on.

As he scrambled to a higher rock ledge, he ducked back down and motioned me to quickly join him. And as I pushed myself up the next steep, slippery section, finally sagging down beside him, I hoped and prayed the animals would still be there when I peered over the ridge.

"Look! Over the rocks!" he whispered with excitement.

I crept forward, slowly craning my head to look. And amazingly, some two hundred yards away, were two of the largest gemsbok I had ever seen. Best of all, they didn't have any idea we were there! My heart was pounding as these gorgeous animals contentedly grazed among a small patch of green on the mountainside.

"Get your breath, steady your breathing, and acquire the target," my guide urgently whispered.

I know. This is what I had worked hard to prepare for, and I was determined not to waste such an available window of opportunity.

"The one on the left is a very, very nice one," whispered one of the South African trackers who was with us.

"Yes," my guide directed, "take the one on the left when you are ready. You're going to be glad you made the extra effort and worked so hard to be ready for this moment!"

I steadied my breathing, brought the scope to my eye, took one deep breath, exhaled, then another, and then with half of it expelled, I squeezed the trigger.

Nothing can describe the internal feeling of exaltation and celebration as I watched that magnificent animal crumple, hit the ground, and start rolling down the mountainside. I burst up from my sniper's perch, both hands thrust into the air in triumph, and started high-fiving everyone in sight! The preparation had enabled the execution, which ended in unrestrained celebration.

Every hunter and fisherman knows what I'm talking about. Something you have worked hard for, imagined, dreamed about, and accomplished—*what a feeling!*

As I gazed at my trophy, I was reminded of what it took to bring that moment to fruition: travel, preparation, exercise and workouts, license, days of effort, saving money for the trip. The truth is, nothing worth accomplishing and experiencing in life comes easy. It requires effort, focus, commitment, persistence, and follow-through.

And sometimes, a lot of climbing.

That includes living a life of faith as well. It's what Paul meant when he told Timothy: "Soldiers don't get tied up in the affairs of civilian life . . . and athletes cannot win the prize unless they follow the rules. And hardworking farmers should be the first to enjoy the fruit of their labor" (2 Timothy 2:4–6, NLT). The goal of being strong in Jesus draws us forward, and all the hard work takes us somewhere that the lazy and unmotivated can never reach.

So here are a few things to ponder: Are you spending as much effort preparing to live your life effectively as a Christ-follower as you are in preparing for your next fishing and hunting expedition? Is your focus as intent on being a "trophy of grace," reflecting the character of Christ in your life, as on getting a trophy for your wall?

Do you know what all this climbing is for? And why it is so worth it?

⊕ Taking Aim

1. What are two steps you can take now to be a more disciplined follower of Jesus Christ?

2. What are you currently climbing that's wearing you out, making you wonder if you can make it to the top? What will most likely happen if you stop now?

- - -

Lord, keep me climbing.

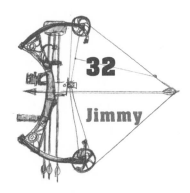

REVERSING
THE RHYTHM

The grace of God that brings salvation has appeared to all men. It teaches us to say "No" to ungodliness and worldly passions, and to live self-controlled, upright and godly lives. (Titus 2:11–12)

I was sitting in the duck blind next to the Duck Commander himself—Phil Robertson. Maybe you've seen his TV show, *Duck Dynasty*, on the A&E Network. His son Jase was to my right, along with two of the other Duck Men—Mac Owen and John Godwin—and my friend Bill McDonald. We were deep in the Louisiana swamp in Phil's flooded woods, on a hole he affectionately calls The Burn, experiencing a temporary lull in the action. During such down times, the conversations in the blind usually center around one of two topics: ducks or God.

"As far as I'm concerned, it's God, family, and ducks, in that order," Phil said in a summarizing voice, as he did a thumbs-up with one hand and shook it.

I've heard it said that since humans have two ears and one

mouth, we should listen twice as much as we speak. I decided to heed that advice.

"Sites, too many people who call themselves Christians are missing the boat," Phil continued. "They think they have to perform well to get God to like them and accept them."

At that moment I noticed the empty shotgun shells that lined the wooden floor of the rustic blind. I reached down and picked up two twelve-gauge hulls—a red one and a black one.

"Here's the way they see it," I responded to Phil's comment.

I held the black shell in my left hand, and the red shell in my right hand. "The black shell represents all their good deeds—their works. If they can do enough of those, then it leads to the red shell that stands for God's grace through the blood of Christ. If they can do enough good works, then they *earn* the grace of God and are accepted by Him and saved eternally. But the only outcome of this formula is guilt, because deep down inside, these people know they can never be good enough to merit the grace of God."

Phil's gaze moved from the shotgun shells in my hands, to my eyes, then to the sky, and then back to the shells again, "Go on, Sites."

I continued, "When we think this way, I believe we are reversing the rhythm. To correct it, we need to move the red shell to the left hand, and put the black shell in the right hand. We *start* with the red shell—the one that represents the grace of God. We are saved because of God's grace, in spite of the fact we don't deserve it. As a result, we then do works for God because we're so thankful that we're saved. The outcome of *this* formula is joy and peace."

The Duck Commander stopped looking at the sky and fixed his gaze on the two empty shotgun shells. He then looked directly in my eyes and said, "I like it, Sites. I like it!"

Take a look in your own life. Do you have the black shell before the red shell, thinking you need to get everything right and be a super-spiritual person in order for God to forgive you and save you? Or do you have the red shell before the black one, gratefully receiving God's grace in spite of your sinfulness, then living every day with great joy because you *get* to do wonderful things for the One who loves you dearly and has already saved you?

You can either look at it as a *got* to, or you can look at it is a *get* to. One is focused on *law*; the other is focused on *love*.

Have you reversed God's rhythm? Make sure you have your empty shotguns shells in the right order.

 **Taking Aim**

1. Paul wrote in Galatians 2:16, "A person is not justified by the works of the law, but by faith in Jesus Christ. So we, too, have put our faith in Christ Jesus that we may be justified by faith in Christ and not by the works of the law, because by the works of the law no one will be justified." What does that tell you?

2. Circle the words "works" and "faith" in the passage above. Notice that they appear in the same order as the shotgun shell analogy found within this chapter. At the beginning of the verse, the word "works" comes before "faith," but at the end of the verse the proper rhythm is restored, with "faith" coming before "works."

3. Consider creating a plaque or a drawing with this verse inscribed on it. Attach a red shotgun shell and a black shotgun shell to the plaque. It might be labeled "God's Perfect Rhythm."

4. Which is the better outlook on life? And why? (circle one)

GOT TO **or** GET TO

- - -

Lord, thank You for grace.

33

Bob

KEEPING THE
RIGHT THINGS HOT

*Because you are lukewarm—neither hot nor cold—I am about
to spit you out of my mouth. (Revelation 3:16)*

There are some things in life I just do not like: sand in my swim trunks, some foreign object in my eye I can't get out, a nagging cough.

There are even a few things I find hard to like about hunting, such as a frigid, blustery morning in a deer stand, shaking from cold, the wind whipping and blowing right through me. Sometimes I find myself wondering, "What am I doing here?"

But I stumbled onto a great discovery concerning this cold-weather issue. A few years ago, I had an agonizing back problem in the 5–7 vertebra area. Doctors put me on a no-work regimen (which is not all bad, I admit)! All I could do was sit still, not move around too much, and sleep sitting up at night in an oversized recliner (which *is* all bad)! I had rarely experienced pain like that.

And when I wasn't adhering to the doctor's orders of a passive agenda, I was undergoing therapy designed hopefully to avoid surgery, combined with medical treatments to reduce the swelling in the spinal column.

It was during this time that I discovered *heat wraps*, which can be purchased at a drug store or the pharmacy area of a discount center. When unwrapped and velcroed around the body's trunk, these handy items produce heat consistently for a number of hours, helping the body relax and repair. They've created wraps for the neck area, as well, which use adhesive ends to keep them in place at the base of the neck and to accomplish the same purpose.

Months later, after vast improvement to my back, I began to wonder, "Why couldn't these same wraps be used to keep my body warm on a cold day of hunting?" And so my experiments began. And the results were beyond my hopes.

Whenever I am facing a day of hunting anymore in which the weather is predicted to be cold and windy (thereby exacerbating the cold), I make sure to pack both kinds of thermo wraps, one for my back and one for my neck. And they have never let me down.

This experience has reminded me of the importance of having heat in the right places. Jesus spoke to the church at Laodicea and said, "You are neither cold nor hot, but lukewarm, and I will spew you out of my mouth." The believers there had lost the heat of their love for Jesus Christ and of their service to Him. They were halfhearted in their relationship with Christ and most likely with each other. And that made Christ want to, well . . . throw up.

Remember, as the Christian movement spread in the first century, followers of Christ were first called "Christians" in Antioch, the church that became the launching pad for Paul's missionary journeys to the world. That word—*Christian*—meant "Christ ones" or "little Christs." In other words, these were people with the same abandonment to the call and will of God that Christ had evidenced in His own life. They were *surrendered* followers, not simply followers whenever convenient.

One of the mentors in my life, in his later years, was Dr. Bill Bright, founder of Campus Crusade for Christ. I well remember every time I would prepare to say good-bye to him, I would ask him what I could pray for on his behalf. His answer never varied: "Pray that I will never leave my first love, Bob. Pray that the heat of my love for Christ and my obedience to His Word would never waver."

So the question begs to be asked: "What is the function of heat? Just to be warm?" Absolutely not! When applied to an injury, heat is meant to restore the body's ability to accomplish its purpose and carry out its mission. In the case of a hunt on a cold day, heat allows the body to function to its best capacity, executing the skills needed to accomplish a successful hunt. Heat is a means to the end, not the end in itself. Heat leads to an appropriate action.

So let me ask you, how is the "heat" of your love for Christ? Is it intense? Is it evident? Does your passion radiate to those around you? Do those in your family see it clearly? How about those who work beside you? What about the people with whom you socialize and recreate? Does the heat of your passion propel you to achieve God's purpose?

Here's a question a guy once asked me that rocked my world: "Bob, if you were put on trial as to whether you were really and truly a surrendered follower of Christ, would there be enough evidence to convict you, based on the evident heat of your passion for Christ?" That one stopped me in my tracks. How about you?

I mean, who wants to be guilty of making Christ want to throw up? Yet that's exactly what it says in the Scripture—people who are so lukewarm in their surrender to Him, they make Him sick at His stomach.

Do you need to take your commitment up a few notches? Does it need to be more evident? Wouldn't you prefer for your life to bring Christ a satisfied smile rather than a sick stomach?

 **Taking Aim**

1. What are you doing to keep the "fire" of your relationship with Christ "hot" in your life?

2. Do the people around you clearly see the "heat" of Christ in your life? And does it affect their life? How?

- - -

Lord, fire me up.

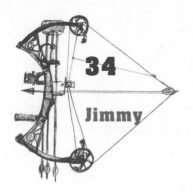

34

Jimmy

FORBIDDEN FRUIT

There is a way that appears to be right, but in the end it leads to death. (Proverbs 14:12)

A thought came to my mind the other day when I was in one of those deep, reflective moods about life. Here's the thought: *everyone has a forbidden fruit.*

I often speak at wild game dinners and tell the story of Eve in the Garden in Eden. She had only one rule to live by: "You must not eat from the tree of the knowledge of good and evil" (Genesis 2:17). That was it. One single don't in a whole, wide paradise of "do whatever you wants."

Wouldn't that make life easier if we, like Eve, had only one rule to live by?

But think seriously about this. You and I may really only deal with one primary, forbidden fruit in our lives—the one thing that tempts us and trips us up more than anything else. No doubt, it's a very tempting fruit. It can easily become so all-consuming, it's often the first thing we think about when we wake up and the last thing we think about before we go to sleep. We find ourselves wanting to be in its presence, even if we know it's bad for us. As a result, we end up doing the same thing as Eve in the garden, going in search of that one forbidden fruit, even taking it in our hand, taking it to our lips, taking it into our bodies.

We know this is true. We know this can happen. So what do we do?

What will *you* do?

First, be honest with yourself as to where you are in the process. Sometimes the simple act of identifying your forbidden fruit—getting it out in the open, writing it down—can start tarnishing its power and appeal.

1. Name the fruit: _____

2. How often do you think of it? _____

3. Have you gone in search of it? _____

4. Have you touched it? _____

5. How have you indulged in it? _____

If you have moved past #4 and participated in #5, you know you've gone too far. You're already feeling the effects of violating God's law and are dealing even now with the implications of sin—perhaps not so visibly at the moment, but give it time. The implications will come.

Hopefully, however, you've already had enough. You can see where this is taking you, your family, and others, and you know this can't go on. You don't want this forbidden fruit in your life anymore. You just want whatever it takes to get it out.

Then the first thing you need to do is ask God to forgive you, as well as any other person you may have harmed with your sin. Then you need to get rid of any fruit that is still remaining. Stop making trips to the tree. Ask others to help hold you accountable to stay away from the fruit. And commit to honoring God for the rest of your life on earth.

If you have not yet arrived at #5, now is a great time to seek the Lord and ask for His help in your overall "forbidden fruit prevention" plan. One of his most effective measures, like I just mentioned, comes from seeking the assistance and friendship of others who can participate in holding you accountable—people who can walk with you closely enough so you avoid the tree altogether, no matter how tempting the fruit is.

Will it be easy? No! In order to ask for help in this way, you will need to overcome pride—the pride that says, "I can do this myself." Remember what Scripture says: "Pride comes before destruction, and an arrogant spirit before a fall" (Proverbs 16:18).

You may try to rationalize by saying, "If I tell somebody else about my struggle, then they will think less of me. They'll always think I'm struggling with this for the rest of my life." Well, which is worse—not telling somebody and ending up eating the fruit, or telling them and dealing with far lesser implications (which probably won't be negative anyway—only positive, helpful, and encouraging)?

Is fruit sweet? Absolutely. Sin is very pleasurable. But the pleasure doesn't last. The fruit becomes bitter. It rots, leaving disease and devastation in its path.

If you don't believe that, ask Eve. She lost her perfect garden and was banished from it forever. She was left to endure increased pain in childbearing, always living with her guilt or at least the memory of it. Death came into her world. And though God forgave her and blessed her in many other ways, she still died because of eating the fruit.

Be honest about your forbidden fruit. Is it really worth it?

Taking Aim

1. What is your definition of sin?

2. Paul says in Romans 3:23, "All have sinned and fall short of the glory of God." Why is mankind so inclined to sin?

3. Read James 1:13–15. Now create your own chart displaying the progression of sin as revealed in these verses.

4. Write down the name of an adult you trust who might serve as your accountability partner (or the person who is already doing so). Call them and let them know of your desire to get rid of any forbidden fruit in your life.

- - -

Lord, help me say no.

35

Bob

REFUELING STATION

The heavens declare the glory of God; the skies proclaim the work of his hands. (Psalm 19:1)

They call it Big Sky for a reason!

And you only have to be there once to understand.

On clear days the panoramic spectacle of blue surrounds you, and the view seems to reach forever. Stretching across Gallatin and Madison counties in Montana, located approximately midway between West Yellowstone and Bozeman, this area known as Big Sky features a beautiful valley nestled within the mountains called simply "The Meadow," an alpine ridge initially called the Gallatin Canyon Basin. It's home to two large ski resorts that tumble down from "The Mountain" sector: Big Sky Ski and Summer Resort, as well as Moonlight Basin.

Part of the Big Sky footprint along the Gallatin River is also a favorite for white water rafters and kayakers. Named after Albert

Gallatin, U.S. Secretary of the Treasury during the Lewis and Clark Expedition, this sparkling body of water is a renowned trout stream that attracts fly-fishers from around the world.

I know firsthand because I have been privileged to stand in those waters—and to forget for a while about all my schedules, pressures, and deadlines. It was something I truly needed. It's something we *all* need.

To enjoy a sense of Sabbath.

Cheryl and I, along with our dear friends Beth and Steve, once spent several days in this wonderland of beauty and awesome ruggedness. Each day in the early morning hours, as well as in the fading hours approaching dusk, we were involuntarily glued to the picture windows of our cabin, scanning our binoculars across the topography stretching before us. We had seen deer, wolves, a bear, even some eagles. We had feasted on the amazing creation of God, all against a sloping range that merged into a backdrop of forest, continually unfolding as far as the eye could see.

Having allowed ourselves the freedom to settle into these restful pleasures, someone eventually had the idea: "Let's go fly-fishing." So off to the outfitters we headed. Getting into our waders was a bumbling procedure that should have been captured on *America's Funniest Home Videos*. And stepping into the rushing waters was a carefully precipitous maneuver, knowing that if we slipped and fell, we would end up with the river flowing *inside* our waders rather than *outside*. But standing there with our fly rods, looking around at the glistening scenery, listening to the mix of quiet and natural motion, watching the snow clouds moving in over the mountains—it was truly a sight to behold.

As we settled into the rhythm of casting, reeling, and casting again, the snow suddenly began to fall, creating a *Currier and Ives* moment as we stood in the river, surrounded by mountains on all sides, staggered by the profound beauty and peace. Suddenly all of the cares of life fell away as though being absorbed and swept along in the river and the gentle snowfall. Our eyes consumed the picture-perfect landscape around us. Smiles spread across each of our faces. We couldn't stop expressing our sense of wonder, thanks, and unadulterated joy.

We all need moments like that.

But I must admit, I don't take enough of them. Quite the opposite, in fact. Sometimes when I relax, I feel guilty. In our Energizer Bunny culture, we are often driven to believe that if we're not constantly busy, something must be wrong, we're not pulling our weight, we're leaving things undone. *Productivity* is not just a corporate term, but an individual term of worthiness on a moment-by-moment basis.

So we can identify with the extremely successful man—the person everyone looked up to with a touch of envy—who privately broke down to his pastor in tears one day, saying, "I can't take it much longer. The expectations keep mounting, even though most of the things expected of me are beyond me control. The demands keep building, the calendar keeps filling, and I keep falling further and further behind. I don't know how much longer I can keep up the image of having it all together."

This is exactly why God established the law of the Sabbath. He built into life the expectation to walk away and be refueled. He knew it was critical for our spiritual, emotional, and physical health and balance. He didn't mean it as an option, but rather as a way of life. So how did we get so far off track?

At points when the pressures of life are mounting, when the expectations are unrelenting, when the demands of the calendar are building, when the weariness is growing, we all need a break. And you don't have to go to Big Sky to do it (although going there surely isn't a bad idea)! The break moments can come from something as simple as jumping into the car or truck and visiting a state or national park. Or taking a drive away from the city into a peaceful, rural areas. Or heading to one of the thousands of hiking trails dotting our great nation. Just refocusing our lives! Taking some moments to reflect on God's creation, given as a gift for our enjoyment, balance, and protection, is good medicine for the soul.

If you haven't tried it recently, why not today . . . or at least this week? It could be a true game changer!

Taking Aim

1. In the hectic pace of increased demands, busier and busier schedules, and higher expectations, how are you building margin into your life?

2. What activity (or lack of activity)—separate and distinct from what you do all the time on a daily basis—refuels your batteries better than anything else? What is that one thing, when you finally stop to enjoy it, that makes you ask yourself, "What took me so long to do this?"

3. What do you think the following statement means to you personally? "If your output exceeds your intake, your upkeep will become your downfall."

- - -

Lord, slow me down.

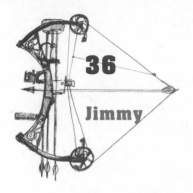

36

Jimmy

TORNADOES
AND PRAYER

We know that in all things God works for the good of those
who love him, who have been called according to his purpose.
(Romans 8:28)

Recently I was turkey hunting with John Carter Cash, son of
legendary musicians Johnny and June Carter Cash. It was our
first day to hunt together, and we only had two days to get the
deed done.

The weather appeared nasty that morning. *Very* nasty! The
brunt of the storm was only two hours away, and high winds were
predicted along with drenching rain. But going against my better
judgment, we hopped in the truck anyway and headed for the top
of the ridge to a listening point where we could await the break
of dawn.

The wind was already howling, and it was very difficult to
hear any gobblers sounding off at my owl hoots. Little did we know

that one of the most horrific tornadoes ever to sweep through the United States was within ninety miles of us. It ended up claiming 337 lives—the second deadliest tornado outbreak in U.S. history to that date.

Every time a tornado hits, I am reminded of a Sunday night years ago when my kids were little. I was preaching in Mountain View, Arkansas, a quaint little town in the northern Ozarks. After the evening worship assembly, several families went to a local soda fountain to have hot dogs and ice cream. My kids, who were playing nearby on a second-floor balcony, suddenly came running down the stairs, screaming "Tornado!" Sure enough, a giant twister was passing just north of town, starting to howl like a freight train.

Not far away, just across the White River, a man named Buddy Brooks, one of the members of the church where I was preaching, was sick in bed inside his log home. Getting up to answer the phone in the kitchen, he happened to look out the window just as the tornado was jumping an adjacent mountain, parting the river-bed at the bottom. The next thing he remembered, he was waking up underneath a pile of rubble. His house had been demolished, though he himself (thankfully) had been strafed with only minor cuts and bruises.

Across the lane from Buddy were his best friends, Larry and Jenny Carney. Rumor has it they were planning to go a local church on Sunday night to be baptized. Jenny, however, came down with a severe migraine, so Larry stayed home with her. Buddy, wandering around in shock, saw both of their lifeless forms lying near their front yard, with only a concrete slab remaining where their house once stood.

The Carney's daughter, Brenda, got the bad news by phone. She had already endured one other significant tragedy in life. Her son Zack had been dropped on his head as a baby in a bath-time accident six years earlier, suffering severe brain damage. He had survived, but not without complications. Her marriage, however, had not. Brenda's husband had never been able to come to terms with the accident, and their relationship ended in divorce. Several years later now, Brenda was left to suffer through yet another painful ordeal—the loss of her parents—without a husband, only the help of her boyfriend.

I recall Amanda and I staying the night in Mountain View, spending the entire next day going through the rubble of Mr. Brooks' house and dealing with reporters who came to take pictures and conduct interviews. Seven people died in that tornado, and many houses were destroyed.

I remember gathering with a group of people to pray that evening. We didn't really know what to say, other than to ask God to be faithful to what He promised in Romans 8:28, that He would make "all things"—even this horrible thing—somehow work out "for the good of those who love him, who have been called according to his purpose."

God really can do that, you know.

He does answer that prayer.

Four years after the Mountain View tornado, for example, I watched as a man led his football team to a Super Bowl championship. He was a man so radically changed by the saving work of Jesus Christ, I remember watching him kneel down during that game beside an injured player from the opposing team—right there on national television—and pray for God to help this fallen warrior endure the pain and recover.

I remember, too, that when a food manufacturer, seeing a chance to benefit from his celebrity, created and marketed a brand of breakfast cereal named after this All-Pro quarterback,

he donated all his proceeds from sales of the product to Camp Barnabas, a Christian camp in Purdy, Missouri, for children with special needs.

During a speaking engagement not long after the Super Bowl victory, he said to a crowd of forty thousand people, "I'm not a football player. That's just what I do. When I throw a touchdown pass now, my thoughts are on how can I use this success on the field as a platform to glorify and praise my Lord Jesus Christ. People often ask the secret of my success as a football player. It has nothing to do with how I work out in the offseason or my diet. The secret of my success is simply Jesus Christ." And to this day, when people ask for his autograph, this ex-Pro Bowler hands them a special trading card he's printed up which tells the story of his conversion to Christ.

The man's name, you may have guessed, is Kurt Warner, former quarterback of the St. Louis Rams and Arizona Cardinals. During his amazing football career, he captured the attention of the whole world. Many children, teens, and even adults idolized him, mimicking his every move. He drew his share of critics and detractors, as well, like people of sincere faith in Christ are sure to do. But I'm thankful for sports heroes like him who stand up for Jesus in the public eye without blinking away from their testimony.

And how does Kurt Warner and the Super Bowl connect to the story of a deadly Arkansas tornado? Because the boyfriend Brenda was dating at the time of her parents' death was none other than Kurt Warner. And because of the faith she displayed in dealing with the grief and suffering of this unexpected crisis, Kurt gave his life to Jesus three months after the tornadoes hit.

"In all things, God works for the good of those who love him, who have been called according to his purpose."

Like I said, God answers prayer.

151

Taking Aim

1. Check the box of the statement below that you believe:

   ☐ God sends tragedy so that He can do some good things as a result of it.

   ☐ God is not the cause of tragedy, but He uses it to do good things as a result.

2. Name one positive thing that God has done in your life as a direct result of a tragedy.

3. Reflect on Brenda's role in the conversion of her boyfriend, Kurt. Is there someone with whom you have an influence that might be won over to God through your lifestyle? If so, who?

4. Read Hebrews 2:9–10 and 14–18. Jesus Christ suffered and died in a tragic way so that you could have eternal life in heaven forever. His is the greatest story of all in terms of good things emerging from tragic circumstances. Say a prayer right now and thank Him for doing that for you.

- - -

Lord, You're too good.

THE REAL DEAL

A new command I give you: Love one another. As I have loved you, so you must love one another. By this all men will know that you are my disciples, if you love one another. (John 13:34–35)

They say the easiest way to detect forged bills is to know the marks of a genuine bill so well that a forgery is obvious. The key is being able to spot the "real deal."

And so is this true in so many areas of life.

As one example, I love to speak at men's conferences and wild game dinners. Nothing quite fuels my fire more than speaking eternal truth to men and watching God dramatically impact their life. And when I do, I've found that the use of visuals really brings these presentations alive, since we're living in such a media-saturated society.

Not long ago, I was privileged to be one of the speakers at a men's conference which drew over five thousand men per weekend for two consecutive weekends. Having been given space for a display of my speaking ministry, I decided to take a few of my mounts to attract attention.

Mounted behind me in that space was a massive black wildebeest and a gorgeous impala which I had taken in South Africa. Then at one end, I positioned my prize: a huge kudu bull with majestic curled horns and a spectacular profile. I was amazed at how the men flocked to see it.

But I noticed a very clear distinction. Some men would gather around, look, shake their head in admiration, and offer a statement of appreciation and congratulations. Those were the *real hunters*. The others would gather, ask permission to get their picture taken with the mount, then stand beside it with their chest proudly puffed up, leaning in with a huge grin on their face while a buddy took their picture. Then they would switch places, and another picture would be snapped. Those were the *wannabe hunters*.

The real hunters didn't need a picture of my prize animals; the wannabe hunters knew that was probably as close as they'd ever get to one.

So I really had to chuckle when later that year, some family members from out of state were visiting our home for a special event. Wanting to see my mounts that they had heard me tell about, we headed downstairs. The oohs and aahs resounded through the basement, especially as certain ones of them—the ones I knew had never hunted before—wanted their picture taken with the kudu. How amazed I was later when that shot showed up on their Christmas card as part of their family photo collage! As good as the picture looked, you could just tell that when it came to real hunters, they weren't the real deal.

Jesus said there would be a surefire way to determine who was the real deal when it came to identifying genuine followers of Christ: a radical difference in how they relate to others. The issue of their authenticity would not be determined simply by how they looked on the outside, or who they hung around with, or what kinds of environments they frequented most often. Their love for others would prove what their spoken profession could only advertise.

Going to an airport doesn't turn a person into an airplane. Being in a garage doesn't make someone a car. Standing around impressive mounts—or even having your picture taken with one—doesn't classify someone as a hunter or fisherman. And the same is true in matters of faith. Simply attending church or having a Bible on the shelf doesn't make someone a Christian. The outward look is not what's critical; the inward transformation is what's essential.

That's exactly what Jesus was getting at when he said that a true, indisputable indicator of a Christ-follower is how they treat others. They will be characterized by a spirit of grace and love. When forgiveness is needed, they will grant it rather than withhold it. When confrontation is needed, they will administer it with sensitivity, not simply with authority. They will understand the difference between permissiveness and boundaries. And they will be willing to give the benefit of the doubt wherever possible. In other words, the proof will be in the pudding. People will see Christ in them, their actions, and their attitudes as they deal each day with those around them.

Do people see that kind of authenticity in you? It's not something you or I can simply work up. It's not merely found in trying harder. It's about allowing Christ to change you and transform you from the inside out. It's the difference between standing around mounts, trying to look like a hunter or fisherman, and actually *being* a true hunter or fisherman.

Don't settle for secondhand experience. Be the real deal.

 **Taking Aim**

1. If you are honest with yourself, do you feel as if the people around you—even those who see you behind closed doors—see Christ evidenced in you, especially by how you treat them?

2. Is there an area in your life that has served as a roadblock, keeping you from experiencing the transformation of Christ within you? What is it? What needs to be done to remove it?

3. Would you pray now, asking Christ to increasingly, daily make you the real deal as a Christ follower—and that others would see it in you?

- - -

Lord, make me real—the real deal.

38

Bob

TAKING AIM AT WHAT'S IMPORTANT

My heart is set on keeping your decrees to the very end.
(Psalm 119:112)

Learning any new skill is tough.

Remember when you were a kid, learning to ride a bicycle? Or when you began to perfect the skill of effectively hitting a target? Remember being a teenager and going through driver's education? Or being a student learning the laws of math or English? (Sorry, didn't mean to bring up bad memories!)

Any new skill takes a lot of work and practice . . . but not just *any* kind of practice. It takes the *right kind* of practice—practicing the right thing in the right way.

How well I was reminded of this reality when I decided to take up bow hunting a couple of years ago. Having purchased my bow and arrows, as well as a good sight and all the supportive equipment, I headed out to do some target practice. I knew enough to realize that when taking up archery, you don't start hunting right out of the gate; instead, you start out at the target range. It didn't take me long, however, to discover I had no idea about the fine points of effective bow shooting. My shot patterns covered anywhere from one-foot-wide distribution to far worse.

That's when Bill entered my life. Bill is an outstanding archer, competitive shooter, and teacher. When I expressed to him that I wanted to learn how to shoot with more consistent accuracy, he asked me how serious I was. Without hesitation, I assured him I would pay the price. So taking me at my word, we set up a date to meet at the range where he teaches.

From watching my first pattern of shots, Bill immediately recognized that he had his hands full. I remember he just smiled and simply said, "We've got some work to do."

His targets were Olympic size on large field stands, spaced at thirty, forty, fifty, sixty, and seventy yards. As we lined up on the thirty-yard target, he had me shoot approximately ten shots. Smiling at my wide distribution, he looked at me and said words I've never forgotten: "Aim small, miss small." With that he walked to the target and removed it from the back stand, replacing it with a four-inch strip of duct tape. When he stepped back to my location, he said, "Now, take a shot at that."

I was stunned when my grouping ended up being between five and six inches wide. Reading the astonishment on my face, he simply said, "See, you were looking at too big of a target. You needed to sharpen your focus. If you aim large, you miss large. But if you aim small, you miss small!"

Focus is the key. Yes, seeing the big picture is an important capacity to use and develop, but when it comes to hitting the target, focus is everything.

That's what the psalmist is saying in today's Scripture. He "set his heart"—that is, he set his focus on what was really important. His concentration narrowed the target, whatever it was, and he blocked out all other things. He knew we can't focus on everything at once; we need to choose a target.

This truth is solid gold, not only in archery or rifle shooting, but in life in general. Proper focus significantly determines how "on target" a person's life is.

What are some areas where you need to refine your focus? Perhaps . . .

- Rather than simply saying, "I need to be stronger spiritually," do you need to start memorizing one Scripture verse per week?
- Instead of griping about your waist, do you need to start a diet and exercise program this week?
- Rather than wishing you were better at showing your wife how special she is, why don't you make a date with her right now for this week, planning to do something you know she'd enjoy?
- Do you wish your kids wanted to spend more time with you? Tell them something you want to do with them this coming weekend. And be sure it's something you know they will love.
- Do you want to get more satisfaction from your work? This week, see how much you can help others experience satisfaction in theirs. You'll be amazed at how much satisfaction will come back to you and how your own contentment will grow.

Be careful not to get hung up on trying to change everything at once. Instead, just take a couple of things at a time, focus on those, and get them where they need to be. Only then should you move on to other targets. Aiming small (with specific, intentional focus) will produce much greater accuracy in your living.

Remember, a long journey begins with a single step. What single step do you need to take?

 **Taking Aim**

1. What are one or two areas in your life that you want to see changed, improved, or strengthened in the next year?

2. What are two specific things in each area that you desire to change?

3. How will you know that the change has occurred? List specific, measurable goals.

- - -

Lord, keep me on target.

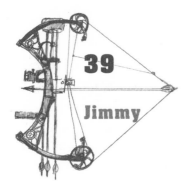

39

Jimmy

AND THEN
JONAH PRAYED

From inside the fish Jonah prayed to the Lord his God. (Jonah 2:1)

I've heard of some crazy things happening to people in the wilds of this world. Like the guy who was scuba diving one bright, sunny day when everything suddenly went dark. A great white shark had approached him from his blind side and attempted to eat him headfirst. The guy's head and torso were actually inside the shark's mouth!

Fortunately the jaws of a great white are not much stronger than a human's, so by swinging and jerking and poking him in the eye, the diver managed to free himself from its grip. The shark followed him all the way to the surface but didn't attack again. Now there's a story to tell around the dinner table!

Speaking of sharks, I was recently fishing on the flats of the Gulf of Mexico near Saint George's Island with my friend Keith Moore. We were wade fishing for reds and specks, and had already come close to our limit on the ten-foot-long floating stringers trailing us down current. I was about two hundred yards away from Keith when I heard his first scream. I looked over to see him flailing the water with the tip of his rod. He was also backpedaling in the waist-deep water, moving faster than I had ever seen anyone move in wading boots.

That's when I noticed the fish head hanging from the end of his rod. I also noticed the six-foot, black-tailed shark that had followed Keith's twenty-inch speckled trout to almost the end of Keith's rod, having grabbed the fish in his jaws, biting off everything but the head. The shark now wanted the rest of his lunch!

As Keith continued to backpedal and scream, he had the presence of mind to remove the fish head from his hook and throw it several feet away. The shark followed it like a dog to a thrown ball. Once again, the victim survives to tell the story.

But there is one fish story I've heard that takes the cake. While it sounds like it must be made up, it isn't. It really happened. The guy's name was Jonah.

Jonah was a Jewish preacher during Old Testament times. He was called by God to leave his homeland and travel to the large, terribly wicked city of Nineveh and preach salvation to the Gentiles.

Naturally, that was about the last thing he wanted to do. He hated the Gentiles. "They're heathens!" he probably responded. "Why would you want them to be saved, God?"

But God insisted. So Jonah started his journey. Only not to Nineveh. Rather, he booked passage on a different boat and headed in the entirely opposite direction.

Not too long into their voyage, however, a great storm brewed and hit. The boat was about to sink. The captain and crew threw off all the cargo in a desperate attempt to keep the vessel afloat, but to no avail. They were all about to sink and drown. Jonah realized the Lord was angry with him about his disobedience, so he told the captain about what he had done and directed the crew to throw him overboard. The captain reluctantly did so and the storm immediately calmed. Meanwhile, a huge fish saw dinner and swallowed it. Jonah found himself in the belly of a whale!

Surrounded by gastric juices and God-only-knows what else, Jonah contemplated his predicament for three long, dark days. The Bible records this story in a book named after him. And the most interesting verse in the book is Jonah 2:1—"From inside the fish Jonah prayed to the Lord his God." Some versions translate it this way: "And then Jonah prayed."

I've thought about this verse many times. Why didn't Jonah pray when God first called him and he didn't want to go to Nineveh? Why didn't he pray while he was on the boat when the storm first hit? In either case the fish incident would have been prevented. But Jonah waited until things had already gone south—way south —before he prayed.

Why do so many people, including myself from time to time, wait to pray until after things go bad?

I told my kids as they were living their teen years, "When you go on a date, pray with the person at the *beginning* of the date, and ask God to help you make the right decisions *during* your date. Then you won't have to be praying *after* your date for God to forgive you for what you did *during* your date." The prayer of prevention is much better than the prayer of conflict management.

If you don't believe it, just ask Jonah.

 **Taking Aim**

1. Can you think of a time when you should have prayed earlier than you did and it ended up badly?

2. Consider your own prayer life. Do you pray more prayers of prevention or prayers of conflict management?

3. Think of something going on in your life right now that needs a prayer of prevention. Write down what that is.

4. Now write or speak a prayer to God asking for His guidance and assistance with what you listed under #3.

- - -

Lord, hear my prayer.

40

Bob

DOES YOUR LIFE SMELL?

For we are to God the aroma of Christ among those who are being saved and those who are perishing. To the one we are the smell of death; to the other, the fragrance of life. (2 Corinthians 2:15)

The morning was cold and overcast. I had been given permission by a friend to slip into some land he owned to bow hunt for a *big* ten-point I had caught a glimpse of a few weeks earlier. His one requirement was that he didn't want me using a tree stand, therefore confining me to the ground. As a result, I had placed my ground blind abutting some woods overlooking a meadow, yet adjacent to a deer trail I had discovered between the bedding area and a beloved food source of deer: persimmons and soybeans.

Being careful, I had sprayed down the blind as I put it up. That morning in the pre-dawn darkness, I had applied some scent-controlling product, dressing in hunting clothes washed in non-scent detergent and dried with specially prepared hunting dryer sheets. I hadn't forgotten to treat my boots and backpack as well.

As the fingers of light crept over the eastern horizon, I was eager with anticipation. Could this be the day? Would the beautiful ten-pointer give me a shot?

I nestled quietly into my blind. I could hear my heart beating as I waited. Surely all my preparation would pay off.

That's when I heard it: the crunch of leaves on the trail behind me. Could it be him?! *Something* was making its way along the path that led between the bedding and feeding areas. And whatever the animal, it was being extremely cautious.

I heard the crackle of a few steps. Then silence. A few more … then quiet again. Then several more cautious steps. That didn't surprise me. After all, bucks don't get big by being stupid!

As I held my breath, the steps drew closer. Louder. Then there was quiet … then a loud snort … then the sound of my big ten-pointer bounding away.

Busted! Who of us hasn't been there? But that doesn't make it any easier to take whenever it happens.

Deer are amazing. They can smell what you and I wouldn't even notice. And there's good reason for that. The normal deer has fifty thousand scent receptors cells per square millimeter of its nose. That's at least four times more than humans. In a steady, gentle wind, they can scent up to a thousand yards across a field. The scent-collecting tissue inside their nose comprises more than a hundred square inches of surface as it folds and wrinkles throughout the nasal cavity. That means even the faintest trace of aroma can be caught by this four-legged smell magnet. Add to this a brain structure that far surpasses a human's in terms of the amount of gray matter devoted to scent detection, and it spells trouble for the hunter!

Believe it or not, the Scripture says God, too, is looking for a scent from our lives. He is seeking a life that, when lived obediently and faithfully to His commands and ways, will create a sweet "smell" rising up before Him. His desire is to sense a man or woman surrendered to His will and striving to please Him in all they do, think, and say. When He finds one, that person gives off a sweet, pleasing aroma that brings a "smile" to His heart. That's the kind of man or woman He chooses to bless.

Let me put it in practical terms any dad can understand. Think of it from the viewpoint of a father and son. When a son obeys his father and walks in the way his father is teaching him to live, the father's heart swells with joy and fulfillment. The satisfaction of seeing his son live well and experience the rewards of obedience far exceeds most any other "scent" he enjoys in life— even the open door of a Krispy Kreme shop filled with the aroma of batches and batches of freshly baked doughnuts . . . and that is saying a lot!

In the same way, our heavenly Father is delighted when He sees our lives (His children) walking in obedience to His Word and ways. He loves it. It brings Him pleasure.

It smells good.

So here is a key question: Do we spend as much effort making our life a sweet smell to God as we do to de-scent ourselves when we're hunting?

As we seek to obey His commands in our daily lifestyle, we show Him just how much we truly love Him . . . or not. That's what Jesus was getting at when he exclaimed, "Whoever has my commands and obeys them, he is the one who loves me. He who loves me will be loved by my Father, and I too will love him and show myself to him" (John 14:21).

So remember, your life is inevitably leaving a scent by the way you are living and obeying your heavenly Father. Is it the scent you really want to leave?

 **Taking Aim**

1. Is there any area in your life where you know there's something you ought to be doing, but aren't?

2. Are there any thoughts you are allowing to stay in your mind that you know would not be pleasing to God?

3. Would God be pleased with your speech, the kind of language you use? Does any of that need to change?

4. What are you going to do about your answer to questions 1–3?

- - -

Lord, help me do something about this smell.

41

Bob

A GUIDE
YOU CAN COUNT ON

I will instruct you and teach you in the way you should go; I will counsel you and watch over you. (Psalm 32:8)

Fall was biting the air, with the crisp temperatures that accompany the season. The leaves were just beginning to change. The aspens' green, coin-sized leaves were tinged with yellow. The hardwoods were giving way to their splendid, multicolored coats that would soon splash the hillsides and valleys with vibrant hues.

My son and I had traveled together for sixteen hours for this experience. He had been overseas for several years (as I'd mentioned before), had fathered twin boys, and was now busily building a career. It had been almost ten years since we'd had the opportunity to walk into the panorama of nature and enjoy sharing a hunt. We had planned this trip for almost a year, so we were expectant, rested, and ready for what the adventure might hold.

We met our guide, Bill, who wore his hunting gear with great ease and exuded the confidence of a man who was comfortable in his own skin. The thought of being led into the hunt by a guy who was this skilled and experienced left us agreeing with each other without saying a word, "This is going to be a GOOD day!"

As we waited in the stark darkness of the lodge a little past 5:30 a.m., Bill began to brief us on the lay of the land we'd come to hunt. He knew it like the back of his hand. Our familiarity with and confidence in our guide grew by leaps and bounds as we listened to him lay out the first day's plan.

He told us that in anticipation of our coming, he had been scouting the elk for a few days. (As seasoned hunters know, patterning is crucial in successful elk hunting, being able to go in already knowing the movements that the elk have been exhibiting during the immediately previous days.) Morning and evening he had searched the dark timber, the bedding areas, and the feeding locations. In anticipation of the rut, Bill had also been noting the movement of the cows. Once the colder weather jump-started the rut, we realized the bulls would go loco, seeking to build their respective harem from among those very cows, while pushing the competitive bulls out.

This was invaluable information. The time he had spent observing and making mental notes was undoubtedly going to pay off for us.

And it wasn't long following his briefing that we were reminded just how important his preparation work had truly been. Within twenty minutes of getting into the field, we were rocked by a jarring bugle that shook us down to the toes of our hunting socks! In the distant mist, we could see the silhouette of a bull making his way along the timber's edge, beginning his trek toward his ultimate bedding area for the day.

Not more than an hour and a half later, after tracking the

elk and their bugles, we suddenly realized we were *surrounded* by bulls, performing an antiphonal chorus around us in a 360-degree circle, crying out and challenging one another. Oh, man—there is perhaps no greater sound than the shrieking, reverberating scream of a bull during rut, letting everyone know, "I'm large and intend to be in charge!"

My son's heart, as well as my own, were pounding at supersonic speeds. I was shocked the elk couldn't hear the throbbing in our chests! This was exactly what we had waited for!

And Bill had known exactly where to lead us, exactly what calls to make, exactly when to move and when not to. It was obvious in watching his every instinct that he had been this way before. He knew exactly what he was doing, and therefore knew what *we* should do. As a result, when he said, "Move!" we high-tailed it in whatever direction he indicated. When he raised his hand up as we made our way through the woods, we froze. When he whispered, "Get ready, I think he'll come in silent," we knew we could take his word to the bank. And later in the hunt, when he would tell us, "This is a bull you want to take a shot at," we were confident from all his prior scouting that he was giving us trusted information. His years of experience in hunting and guiding would pay off in spades, proving invaluable enough to give my son and me a hunt of a lifetime . . . because Bill had been there. And done that. Many, many times before.

Even more important than hunting advice, I find I need excellent guidance in my daily life as well. Spiritually, I need someone who knows the ins and out of life, knows what works and what doesn't, and knows how I can live successfully in every arena. I need someone I can trust and whose word I can take to the bank.

And that is exactly what I find in Jesus Christ—through His

Spirit and through His Word. With Him as our Guide, we can enter every day with confidence and expectation, knowing He will steer us well as we follow His wise instruction.

⊕ Taking Aim

1. Take a moment to pray the words of Psalm 32:8 (printed at the top of today's chapter) and Proverbs 16:9 ("In his heart a man plans his course, but the Lord determines his steps"). Ask God to guide your steps and order your ways.

2. Since Christ has placed the Holy Spirit in your life if you have accepted Him as Savior and Lord, why don't you ask Him to make the Holy Spirit like an internal GPS system in your heart, guiding you to fulfill God's plan for your life?

3. In what ways have you taken control of your own direction in the last three months, not paying sufficient attention to God's direction in your life?

- - -

Lord, lead on.

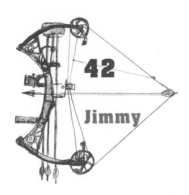

42

Jimmy

BE A NICE GUY ...
SOMETIMES

Watch out for false prophets. They come to you in sheep's clothing, but inwardly they are ferocious wolves. (Matthew 7:15)

Sure, I want to be a nice guy . . . whenever I can. But *nice* isn't always what the various contexts of life call for.

Sometimes, yes, I am far more than nice. Sometimes I do portray love, patience, endurance, sympathy. Sometimes I give kind, gentle, understanding counsel. Sometimes, however, I lean more toward anger and accountability, firmness and rebuke, getting up in someone's face. No tolerance. Sometimes I don't care whether I'm perceived as nice and easygoing or crazy and narrow-minded. Tough.

I'd rather be liked and laid-back, of course, if given a choice. You probably would too. But Christianity is not always so accommodating and comfortable. There is much more to church than having nice, little gatherings.

For several years my family attended a non-denominational church in Franklin, Tennessee, called New River Fellowship. The church was founded by singer/songwriter Michael W. Smith, and when my family starting going, they were in their second year of worshipping together, meeting in a YMCA.

After a few months, Michael approached me about being a teaching pastor on Sundays and Tuesdays. I accepted and launched a series of classes, also taking on some of the preaching. About a year later, Michael approached me once again and asked if I would consider becoming an elder for the church. It would be the two of us serving together.

I listened to his request, all the while feeling the answer "no" forming on my lips. Why so hesitant? Who wouldn't want to serve shoulder-to-shoulder with Michael W. Smith?

Because being an elder—being a leader—often means needing to say things and do things that people don't always think of as nice. Was I ready again for that kind of responsibility? The tough skin? The tense battles?

The main responsibility of an elder is to be a shepherd of the sheep. That's what the original Greek word *poimen* means— "shepherd" or "pastor." For an elder to be a good shepherd, he must smell like sheep. He must spend time with the sheep. He must know them by name and care for them spiritually. He must be willing to take strong action when they cause trouble. He must fight to protect them. He must be willing to do the tough things to keep the sheep safe, not only in the pen but also when they wander away into the wilderness. He must be willing to lay down his life for the sheep.

Look at the experiences of David before he became king of

Israel during the tenth century BC. He was a teenaged shepherd charged with overseeing his father's herd, and he laid his life on the line for those sheep!

Like this: "When a lion or a bear came and carried off a sheep from the flock, I went after it, struck it and rescued the sheep from its mouth. When it turned on me, I seized it by its hair, struck it and killed it" (1 Samuel 17:34–35).

Now you can understand why he wasn't too afraid for action when the Philistine giant Goliath came against him in battle a few years later. He had already been the tough guy for the benefit of the sheep. Now he could be the tough guy for the benefit of the Israelite army and nation.

And what about us? Do we just want to be nice—nice people, nice neighbors, nice Christians? Or do we want to live the way David lived, fighting off the wolves and loving the lambs?

By the way, I eventually said "yes" to Michael's request and embarked on the great adventure of being an elder at New River Fellowship. There were good times and bad, and I was liked and disliked at various intervals by various individuals. Even Michael and I had to have some "sit downs," where we ended up agreeing to disagree on some things. There was laughter and there were tears. There were even a few nights of lost sleep. Such is the nature of being on the heavenly journey with other God-followers. Such is the nature of being part of a family.

It's not as nice as it sounds. Isn't supposed to be.

Can you live with that?

My wife once told me, "Passive men and passionate men don't seem to be the same men. Jesus is a man of passion. You are such a man. It's in your soul. Go for it!" C.S. Lewis also expressed it well: "If you want a religion to make you feel really comfortable, I certainly don't recommend Christianity."

So be a nice guy . . . when you can. But don't back down from the wolves, bears, and giants. And don't tolerate sheep that will lead the flock astray.

⊕ Taking Aim

1. Think of a time when you became aware of evil or danger within your family or church. How did you respond?

2. When is it OK to get angry or confrontational?

3. Read John 2:13–17 and see how Jesus reacted when he was angered by people who were doing wrong. Was he considered a nice guy after that?

4. Now read John 10:7–18. How does Jesus feel about his sheep?

- - -

Lord, keep me sharp.

Bob

LIVING IN
RESPONSE MODE

In your hearts revere Christ as Lord. Always be prepared to give
an answer to everyone who asks you to give the reason for the
hope that you have. But do this with gentleness and respect.
(1 Peter 3:15)

There are times in life when you have to pinch yourself to make sure you're not dreaming!

And on this one particular hunt, I got sore from all the pinching.

Before I returned to South Africa in October 2010, bringing seven friends along with me for a hunting bonanza in some of the most rugged, picturesque land in all the world, I had already been blessed with five wonderful trophies from previous visits. Two of them had been Gold Medal rated (bushbuck, blesbok) and three had come in at Silver (blue wildebeest, impala, and zebra). My experiences there had been better than I could have possibly hoped or imagined, even from when I was a kid watching Tarzan on TV.

This latest adventure had started out with a rugged hunt in

northwest South Africa, with hopes of getting a shot at a long desired goal of mine—a kudu! Spotting a bull, we had maneuvered down jagged mountainsides, only to be forced with scaling another, then crossing over an adjacent ridge. And just as we stopped to catch our breath and plot our next steps, the bottom fell out. A cold, driving rain. We huddled beneath a large aloe vera plant and waited out the storm, praying the kudu wouldn't bolt.

When the rains finally dissipated, we eased along the ridge, where amazingly—not one, not two, but *three* bulls appeared, no more than 175 yards away, eating shrubs, certain they were alone and unobserved.

Two minutes later, despite having to navigate a treacherous, slippery mountainside, my hunting buddy and I had two beautiful kudu on the ground. *Pinch me.*

The week would also produce an impala, a breathtaking black wildebeest, a springbok, and a granddaddy nyala. *Pinch, pinch, pinch.*

Then finally, the last day arrived, and I was ready to pack up and head back to the States, thrilled beyond words. But at 6:30 in the morning, my door was assailed by hard pounding. "Get on some hunting clothes, Bob—quick! The dogs are on the trail of a lynx, and we think it's a big one!"

I had never thought I would get a chance at such an elusive cat—a species the ranchers hate because it's such a killing machine when it comes to livestock. Sized somewhere between a bobcat and a mountain lion, a lynx is fast, cunning, agile, deadly.

And within a matter of frantic, grab-your-gun-and-hang-on minutes, we were hot on its trail, driving like madmen on mountain roads. When the roads could take us no farther, we jumped out of the Land Rover and barreled down the side of the mountain, dodging gigantic thorn bushes that seemed to be grasping for us with every step as we went slipping and sliding after the bellowing dogs.

When we hit the ravine bottom, we sprinted up the other side, evading boulders and heavy underbrush, knowing every minute was crucial. My heart was pounding in my chest; my feet scrambled to stay up with the PH, who was in exquisite shape; and perspiration dripped steadily from my face. But the dogs kept leading us forward, growing louder, until suddenly we broke through some thick undergrowth, and there they were—dancing and jumping below the tree, bellowing at the treed predator.

My eyes shot immediately to the top of the tree, catching just a glimpse of the cat's head as he let loose a shrieking growl, expressing his fury that these dogs had cornered him on this precarious perch. The PH threw the shotgun to my outstretched hands and yelled, "I know you can't see much of him, Bob. He's a big cat! But when you can see some of his body, *shoot!*"—to which he carefully added, "Shoot well, though, because if he comes down wounded, he's going after the dogs. Or us!"

Oh, great. I said a breath-prayer: "Lord, let me be on target!"

Just then, I spotted fur—about the size of a football—and pulled the trigger.

A piercing howl filled the air, and suddenly the lynx was falling from his thirty-foot perch! Thankfully, by the time he hit the ground, we didn't have to worry about him going after the dogs or us. And what a beautiful cat! What a rush! What an end to a hunt!

Suddenly I was pinching myself again, remembering that "every good and perfect gift is from above, coming down from the Father of the heavenly lights" (James 1:17). I began to give thanks for a journey that seemed too good to be true—an experience that reminded me of some key lessons in life:

1. *Great opportunities don't always come with advanced warning and lead time.*

2. *With great opportunity often comes significant risk.*
3. *Sometimes you have to take your best shot, and then deal with what comes.*

These concepts are true not only when hunting in South Africa or even on the South Forty, but also when it comes to talking to others about our faith in Christ. We never know when the situation may arise for us to tell somebody how the Lord has been equal to every need we've ever experienced in life, and how He can do the same for them as well. We may not see the chance coming for us to share how a person can know Christ personally, not just know *about* Him. It takes commitment and preparation, and an eagerness to respond whenever and wherever the opportunity comes.

Be ready for it, though, and you may find yourself in the right place at the right time when God's Spirit is working overtime on someone's heart. I promise you'll go to bed that night pinching yourself to see if you were really there to see it all when that person's whole life turned upside down.

⊕ Taking Aim

1. When God throws an unexpected opportunity in front of you, do you respond quickly and obediently? Or do you think of a bunch of reasons why it wouldn't work?

2. How good are you at taking risk in responding to God's leadership in your life? Or do you want everything predictable, safe, and secure?

3. Where is an area you need to exercise more risk and quick obedience in your life?

- - -

Lord, keep me ready.

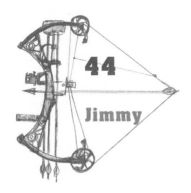

44

Jimmy

HOLY MOMENT ON THE MOUNTAIN

When Moses went up on the mountain, the cloud covered it, and the glory of the Lord settled on Mount Sinai. (Exodus 24:15)

Occasionally someone asks me, "What's the hardest thing you've ever done in the outdoors?" I immediately think of four adventures: 1) living with Stone Age Indians in the Amazon jungle, 2) moose hunting on the Alaskan Peninsula, 3) goat hunting on the cliffs of the island of Kauai, 4) and hunting tahr and chamois on the South Island of New Zealand.

If forced to pick one, I'd have to go with the New Zealand hunt.

If you've seen the movie trilogy *Lord of the Rings*, then you can picture in your mind where my hunt took place. Just think of the rugged, snow-capped mountains behind Aragon as he rides his horse through the rock-strewn river valley after seeing the army of Orcs. I can literally freeze-frame that scene in the film and point to the exact slope where I climbed and shot a huge tahr bull. It was the roughest climb of my life.

Three days later, after my legs had somewhat recovered, I decided to go after the elusive chamois that live at an even higher elevation than the tahr. Only after many hours of climbing did I finally spot two of them across the canyon.

My guide Ian Lowe and I decided to try to get ahead of them at an intersection of ridges in the direction they were walking. We moved as fast as we could, pushing hard until honestly I didn't think I could take another step. Finally we arrived. And waited.

The chamois never showed up.

Ian had the idea that we should climb to the summit of the mountain so we could see better and find them again. My lips said OK, but my legs screamed no! My lips won out, however, and off we went, my two rubbery lower limbs doing the best they could to keep up with the rest of my body as it moved onward and upward.

We finally made it to the summit of one of the tallest mountains in New Zealand. And what an unusual piece of topography it was. A rock about the size of a school bus jutted skyward at the top, as if three-fourths of it had been vertically pushed out of the ground by some unseen force. And after managing to crawl to its crest, my waiting eyes discovered what my weary muscles must have known was worth the effort: one of the most spectacular panoramas I have ever beheld—before or since.

The chamois could wait. I'd found an even greater trophy for the day.

Like I often do at such picturesque moments, I sat down—truly in humble reverence—placed my rifle and backpack beside me, and tried to drink in the full view, simultaneously praising the One who spoke such scenery into existence. Seeing this kind of glory refreshed my soul in ways I didn't even realize needed refreshing until that moment.

For the next two hours, I sat there on top of that mountain. I

prayed. I napped. I reflected on life. I practiced what God encourages us to do in Psalm 46:10—"Be still and know that I am God." And over that course of time, I began to see things in a different light. Inward things. Things of the heart.

I thought about a little boy in Florida named Blake who was fighting for his life against cancer. According to the doctors, he didn't have long to live. Juxtaposing his current experience against what I was encountering in the flesh at that moment—not to mention the wealth of adventures I'd been blessed to enjoy in my half-century of life—my eyes began to water with salty tears, causing me to write the following words in my journal through half-blurred vision:

New Zealand has done something to me on the inside. It is so beautiful! It's like going back fifty years in the United States to a more innocent era. The mountains look so big, but they are even bigger than they look. (Trust me on that one!)

As I sit on the summit of this mountain, I feel that God is whispering to me. I realize the earth really is an amazing place of grandeur and fascination. I have been so blessed to live the years that I've lived and participate in all the adventures that I've experienced. I've got great kids, have known the love of a good woman, and have lived a very fulfilled life. Best of all I have a secure future that's going to last forever. The best is yet to come.

I guess what I'm realizing is that I'm really looking forward to moving on to the greatest adventure of all and living in heaven. I want this more than ever before. I would gladly trade my life for the life of young Blake in Florida.

Lord, if you want to work such a miracle and move my health to Blake, I'll take his cancer. I'll trade my life for his.

You can take me right here on this mountain if you wish. I can't lose either way. Your will be done. I love You, Father.

God didn't accept my offer. Blake passed on a few weeks later. I was thankful to be able to attend his funeral. But that doesn't change the holiness of that moment for me. God's will is done, and that's final. I accept that. My job is to continue living out each day, recognizing that my life depends on the God who lives behind these holy moments.

I think I'm finally starting to understand what I saw in some good ol' country folks who inspired me during my college days. When I first started preaching as a college student at Harding University, I served at a small country church in Enola, Arkansas. Many of the fifty-seven members of that little congregation would arrive at least a half hour before services and sit quietly on a pew. At first I tried to make small talk with them, but it quickly became evident they weren't there to talk. I considered them a bit rude at first, but as I got to know them better, I realized they were simply busy with something much more important than chit-chat—preparing their minds for an incredible event: the *shekinah* of God.

The Hebrew word *shekinah* refers to the glory or radiance of God dwelling in the midst of His people. The root for this word is *sheken*, which appears 129 times in the Old Testament. Out of these dozens of occurrences, God is the subject of the verb forty-three times.

One example is found in the giving of the Ten Commandments in Exodus 24:15–18:

> When Moses went up on the mountain, the cloud covered it, and the glory *[shekinah]* of the Lord settled on Mount Sinai. For six days the cloud covered the mountain, and

on the seventh day the Lord called to Moses from within the cloud. To the Israelites the glory of the Lord looked like a consuming fire on top of the mountain. Then Moses entered the cloud as he went on up the mountain. And he stayed on the mountain forty days and forty nights.

Richard Foster, writing in his classic book *Celebration of Discipline*, says: "To worship is to experience Reality, to touch Life. It is to know, to feel, to experience the resurrected Christ in the midst of the gathered community. It is a breaking into the Shekinah of God, or better yet, being invaded by the Shekinah of God."*

The farmers at the little country church in Enola were preparing themselves for the invasion of God in worship. It was actually no different than what I was seeking and experiencing on top of that mountain on the South Island of New Zealand. Every time we worship Him in spirit and truth—no matter where we are—we open ourselves to the same invasion of God's presence within us.

I'll never forget my holy moment on the mountain.

I want more of them.

Even from elevations way down here.

 **Taking Aim**

1. What do *you* do to prepare yourself for the *shekinah* of God?

2. Mind if I offer a few suggestions?

- Go to bed at a reasonable hour on Saturday night so you'll be refreshed on Sunday to worship with your church family.

- Get up early enough on Sunday morning that you can spend some time reading the Bible and praying that God will prepare your heart and mind for worship . . . and so you don't have to rush to get there.

- When you go to church, arrive at the church building early, enter the auditorium quietly, and sit still. Meditate on the answer to this question: "Who am I here to worship this morning?" (Visiting with your friends can wait till afterward.)

- Humble yourself before God and surrender yourself to Him by singing with all your heart and mind, digging into Scripture with your full attention, and praying in complete submission to His will. Eat and drink in celebration of His death and resurrection in communion. Be awed by God as His *shekinah* invades your worship and radiates through the lives of the worshippers.

- - -

Lord, start the invasion.

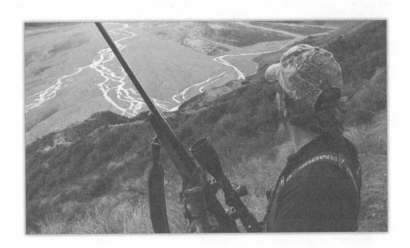

*Richard Foster, *Celebration of Discipline* (Harper San Francisco, 1978), 158.

Bob

IT'S NEVER TOO LATE

The Lord had said to Abram . . . "I will make you into a great na-
tion and I will bless you; I will make your name great, and you
will be a blessing. I will bless those who bless you, and whoever
curses you I will curse; and all peoples on earth will be blessed
through you." (Genesis 12:1–3)

Have you ever thought time had run out on you? That you no
longer had even a slim chance of success? That it was simply
too late for things to work out or come together?

Join the club. You're in good company.

Can you imagine Abram, for example—at seventy-five years
of age—getting a promise from God like the one mentioned
above? I mean, how does an old man with no son, with his child-
producing years a distant memory, go about launching a "great
nation" from his own family tree? Who is God kidding here?

And you—what about the opportunities of life that have

passed *you* by? How do you go back and recapture what you missed? Who do you convince to give you another shot? What's the point of even trying anymore?

My friend Alan might have an answer for you.

We were hunting in South Africa once. It was the last day. The next morning we were scheduled to head out for the airport, leaving no later than 8:30 a.m. in order to catch our connecting flight to Johannesburg, where we would retrieve and recheck our luggage and guns before setting off on a sixteen-hour return flight to the States. If we were late for our first check-in of the day, we risked never catching up with ourselves—or our gear.

This had been Alan's first time in Africa. And while he had loved soaking in the wonder of that amazing country, he had frankly come up short on the animals he had hoped to take. And his time had run out.

My heart ached for him. I could see the disappointment in his eyes—enough that I decided to try one last gasp at salvaging Alan's hunting trip.

Gary, one of the best guides I'd ever worked with—all of twenty-two years old—completely sympathized with the situation when I slipped up to him quietly and asked if he could do anything for Alan. So did Glen Olivier, the safari owner, a wonderful guy and friend. Both agreed we needed to do everything possible to make something happen, even though the clock was working against us.

Around nightfall, Gary told Alan to be up and ready for him before sunrise, that they would head out to be in position when first light broke the next morning. Our *last* morning. They'd give it one more go.

It would've helped, of course, if the *truck* would go. Instead, the next day, it sat there in the early morning darkness, tilted to one side on a deflated, heavy-duty tire, and seeming to take all the air out of Alan's hopes as well. But with the speed reminiscent of a NASCAR pit crew—and the rush of one final hunt hanging in the balance—they quickly changed the tire. And changed Alan's fortunes. Within fifty minutes, he was back in time for our journey home, dragging a big, black wildebeest behind him. He didn't even need a plane to get back to the States; he was airborne already.

But what if they hadn't gone out that one last time? What if they had resigned themselves to failure? What if they'd concluded it was just too late?

I can relate to that.

About three and a half years ago, I sat listening to a conference speaker tell about the amazing experiences he and his son had enjoyed throughout the boy's growing-up years, how they had regularly spent time one-on-one, exploring God's Word together.

I admit—it made me hurt inside. My own son and I had a close relationship as well. We had done a lot of things together when he was younger. And now that he was a grown man and husband, I regularly prayed for him and was so proud of him. But if I was being honest, I'd have to say that about the closest we came to regularly reading the Bible together was with me behind a pulpit and him in the audience. I couldn't escape the fact that I had passed up nearly all my opportunities to truly disciple my son in the Scriptures face to face.

I'll never forget the regret and conviction of that moment.

Because now it was too late.

Have you ever been in a situation where you finally saw the right thing to do—more clearly than ever before—but there wasn't a single thing you could do about it? Not anymore? You had your chance. You missed it. Get over it.

My son was twenty-nine years old at the time. Away from home. Living in a whole other part of the country. Too bad. Too late.

Unless . . .

I remember the day I picked up the phone, no longer able to manage this inner struggle that would not go away, and called his number, not really knowing what to say. I could almost hear Harry Chapin's "Cat in the Cradle" playing in my head, with myself playing the older father who'd too often allowed himself to be too busy to spend quality time with his boy, and my son playing the grown young man, now too busy to make time for his dad.

When he answered, I did my best to explain why I was calling. I told him about what the conference speaker had said. I told him about the regrets I'd been feeling. I told him I was sorry. I told him I hoped he could forgive me.

But somewhere in that somewhat awkward conversation, I stopped telling him things and decided to ask him something. I asked him what he thought about choosing one book of the Bible, or perhaps a Christian book for men, and seeing if we could somehow study it together. Maybe we could read independently each week, and then get on the phone, wherever we were, and just share what God was teaching us as men, husbands, and dads.

That conversation happened more than three years ago. And since that time, my grown son and I have spent some of the most thrilling hours of my life on the telephone, talking, discussing, laughing, confessing, celebrating, learning, growing. Each call has reminded both of us that we are still works in progress. But it sure is easier to handle when you're working it out together. It's been incredible.

In fact, just as I was finishing up writing this chapter, I received a text. My son's work is taking him to the Middle East soon for an extended period of time. And he's wanting to see what

I think about some of the books he's taking with him for us to Skype over while he's gone.

Imagine that.

I almost missed it.

But it's never too late.

 **Taking Aim**

1. Is there any area in your life where you have convinced yourself, "It's too late"? Do you need to reconsider?

2. Why have you been willing to buy the lie that time has run out?

3. What are two things you could be missing because you've quit too soon or have given up too easily?

4. Are you willing to give these things a try? When will you start?

- - -

Lord, please give me another chance.

46

Bob

IN THE ACTION

Do not merely listen to the word, and so deceive yourselves. Do what it says. (James 1:22)

I love action in life, and I've been with Jimmy enough to know he's cut from the same cloth.

I've paraglided off the Swiss Alps, been scuba diving with my son among sharks, hiked the Pecos Wilderness in New Mexico, and babysat my nonstop twin grandsons. (Trust me, that last one is no less an adventure!) Even when I'm wanting to read or study, I almost always prefer to do it with other people around, in a public place, rather than holed up in some quiet, breathless room somewhere, attempting to recreate the mausoleum silence of a library.

So no wonder it's hard for me to face a sixteen-hour flight to Africa, even when I know the privilege of hunting is awaiting me on the other side. Such trips involve an eternity of waiting, traveling, lugging bags, sitting, dozing off, trying to listen to music or watch a movie, more sitting, more waiting. Throw in a delayed flight, an upset stomach, a broken AV system on the plane, or an oversized passenger sitting next to you who takes up not only his own seat but part of yours, and it's amazing what we're willing to go through to exercise our passion for the hunt. (And all of those happened to me on the last trip!) Throw in a lost piece of luggage, and you've got the icing on the cake. And yet we're still willing to cope with it all for the sheer joy of adventure and the possibility of a trophy at the end.

So here's my question: Why will we do all of that to go on a great hunting or fishing expedition—immunizations, customs authorizations, TSA checks, packing for all kinds of weather, sighting in our rifles, relentless practicing, vigorous exercise, getting ahead of our workload so it's not quite as piled up when we return—and yet we often won't make the smallest effort just to walk next door and invite a neighbor to church, or to tell a friend about the difference Christ has made in our life and could make in theirs? Why will we talk with a colleague—or even a perfect stranger—about business, sports, entertainment, vacation plans, and work projects, yet we avoid matters of faith like the plague? We almost never lack for names of people we could possibly ask when we're wanting somebody to go with us to a sporting event, a movie, a concert, or a restaurant. But when it comes to inviting someone to church, our mind seems to go blank . . . or talks us out of every option. Maybe next week. Maybe next time. Maybe next Christmas.

"Maybe never" is more *like* it.

Could it be that we too often buy into an inadequate concept of success and trophy? Perhaps here is the question: When you really consider what is important in life, which is most fulfilling? A fish or animal mount on your wall? Or the transformed life of someone to whom you have been privileged to help introduce to Christ?

Jimmy and I have been blessed to experience both, and we unhesitatingly say there is *no comparison!* Not even close.

So who in your life's network of relationships comes to your mind when you think of someone who needs a personal relationship with Christ? Are they in your family? At work? In the neighborhood? At the club or gym? At school? What effort do you need to invest to move toward the thrill of a lifetime, seeing them come to the point of asking Christ into their life? Like a hunting of fishing trip, it begins with intentionality, moves forward with preparation, requires practice, and takes effort. But the possibilities of reward are beyond words.

Allow me to offer a simple yet profound first step. If you're like me or most other guys I've known, one thing you enjoy is eating. So there's a good chance you probably go out to a restaurant every once in a while. The next time you do, try this: once you've placed your order, stop the waiter or waitress before they scoot away, and tell them, "When you bring our food shortly, we're going to say a blessing for it. When we do, what is one thing specifically we could pray about for you?"

You will be amazed at the doors this one little gesture will open. I have *never*—not once!—had a server refuse or be uninterested in my request, and that's after asking this simple question hundreds of times over the years. It is so easy! And the opportunities it gives to talk openly about Christ is mind-boggling. Try it! I think you'll like it!

Start today, praying for a person by name. Ask God to begin preparing their heart to receive the message, and to prepare your heart to share it. Ask your heavenly Father to open doors of opportunity in the future. And then stay on the lookout for the doors to swing open.

Remember, like a good hunting or fishing expedition, it will take work. But it'll put you out there where the action is.

⊕ Taking Aim

1. What excuses do you find yourself offering when thinking of inviting someone to a Christian event or to church, or about sharing with someone what Christ has specifically done for you?

2. Why do you sometimes find sharing about your faith in Christ more challenging than talking about politics, sports, news, or business?

3. How about getting intentional about inviting a friend to church this month who you know is not actively attending church anywhere? Remember, it is all about intentionality.

- - -

Lord, I want a piece of the action.

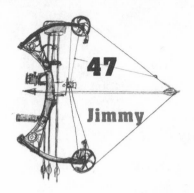

47

Jimmy

MONKEY SEE, MONKEY DO

You have heard that it was said . . . But I tell you . . .
(Matthew 5:43–44)

During my time in the Amazon jungle, I had the privilege of going on a blowgun hunt with Steve Saint and the Waodani tribe's best hunter, Omena.

Two hours before daylight, Steve (whose father, missionary pilot Nate Saint, was slain by this very tribe in this very location in 1956) woke me and said, "Time to go." We loaded into a primitive but very functional dugout canoe and headed downriver, being careful not to go past a certain landmark we were told about: home to a fierce tribe of head-shrinking, cannibal Indians.

We were here to hunt, not to be a hot entrée.

Omena and Steve were at the bow of the dugout while my cameraman Brandon and I sat at the stern. After an hour and a half of travel, I began to see a pink glow on the horizon. My stomach told me it was time for breakfast. I checked my backpack to see if I had any granola bars left. None. Then my hand felt the familiar shape of a small banana. I retrieved it and immediately reached for the stem to peel it.

Just as I began to bend the stem, I remembered something: a paradigm-changing conversation with an African-American man who had visited our home not long before.

Howard, a friend of my father-in-law, Dr. Jerry Mullens, had come to stay with us for a few days. Howard's father was one of the legendary Tuskegee Airmen of World War II, about whom a movie was recently made. As we were eating breakfast one morning, Howard watched me peel a banana and begin eating it. He asked me, "Jimmy, is that the way you've always opened a banana?"

"Yes."

"Why?" he asked.

"Well," I responded, "that's the way I've always done it."

Once again Howard asked, "Why?"

I paused and thought before answering. "I guess that's just what I've always seen other people do."

Howard then reached for a banana in a fruit bowl and proceeded to open it from the opposite end of the stem. I was amazed how easily the banana opened, without mashing the tip or splitting the skin three ways.

He took a bite, chewed, swallowed it, and then said, "If you watch monkeys in the jungle or even at the zoo, you'll see they always open the banana from the end opposite the stem. Many times the banana is still hanging from the tree. The monkey just sits on a limb, reaches up, peels the banana upward, and eats the sweet fruit while the skin is still hanging from the limb. It's the natural way to eat a banana."

I'll have to admit, I was quite impressed by this perspective adjustment. Come to think of it, I can't remember anyone ever verbally teaching me that I should peel a banana by starting with—what else?—the stem. It was just a behavior I had learned by sight and experience. And yet for almost half a century, I had been peeling bananas the "unnatural" way, simply because it was the way I had always seen other people doing it. I never knew there was a better way until Howard actually spoke up and kindly pointed me toward another option to consider.

I guess you could say I've had a banana-peeling paradigm shift. I now almost always open my daily banana in this new way, though at times I forget and revert. I also love to experiment with other people. Often in groups I'll take a quick poll, usually discovering that about 90% of the people open a banana from the stem end. I reveal Howard's information to them, and the reaction is almost always like a light bulb coming on in their heads. I feel like I'm part of a banana-peeling revolution!

Try it yourself. You probably need the potassium anyway.

I can only imagine how many learned behaviors have been in play—in each of our lives, for years—that might actually need to be adjusted or even discarded. Some are harmless, like banana peeling. But others might *not* be so harmless. While it may not come down to a change from wrong to right, it may come down to being *more* effective as opposed to *less* effective. I want to keep an open mind on things like that, don't you? They may actually lead to improvement, whether by shifting the way I think or the way I react to life. Usually these two are joined closely together.

And I'm really not concerned if people think I'm strange or different or a rebel for trying them. If I can learn from a monkey to do something more effectively, then let the monkey be my teacher. Monkey see, monkey do.

I think Jesus had this same thing in mind in the Sermon on

the Mount. In Matthew 5, Jesus delivers six antithetical statements. Basically what he's communicating is: "You have heard it's been said to do it *this* way, but I tell you to do it *that* way."

I encourage you to read the entire fifth chapter of Matthew, and circle these six statements with a pen or pencil. (They're listed in the "Taking Aim" segment below.) Meditate on them and see if there might be a need for a paradigm shift in your own mind related to what Jesus says.

See it? Now do it.

 **Taking Aim**

1. What is something you habitually do, simply because it's what you've always seen others do?

2. Can you think of a more effective or efficient way it might be done?

3. Read the following antithetical statements by Jesus recorded in the Sermon on the Mount. Summarize what Jesus is saying in your own words by writing your answer in the blank provided:

• Matthew 5:21–22 _____

• Matthew 5:27–28 _____

• Matthew 5:31–32 _____

• Matthew 5:33–37 _____

• Matthew 5:38–42 _____

• Matthew 5:43–48 _____

4. The next time you hear someone say, "Because that's the way we've always done it," get a banana and see if you can help that person with his or her perspective.

- - -

Just say it, Lord, and I'll do it.

199

IN SEASON
AND OUT OF SEASON

Be prepared in season and out of season. (2 Timothy 4:2)

Introducing friends to new experiences is a great rush for me. And one of the most exhilarating has been the joy of seeing several meet the intrigue and wonder of the Dark Continent for the first time. Each man isn't quite sure what to expect, but without exception I have watched it surpass their greatest expectation.

In June 2012, I had the privilege of loading up eight friends at the Atlanta airport and heading off on an adventure for which we had planned and prepared for months. A sixteen-hour flight to Johannesburg, an overnight, and on to East London the next morning had us hunting by mid-afternoon.

I had covered the myriad of game with each man, encouraging them to think through and prioritize what species they desired. Each had looked through pictures, dreamed of moments of encounter, ranked their prey, and settled on their plans. But

I had cautioned each of them that in the hunt for Plains game, great unexpected moments with unplanned animals can often arise out of nowhere—sometimes with as little as seven seconds to see the target, acquire it, and pull the trigger. Everyone needed to be ready to make fast judgments on the fly.

Steve is a great friend of some twenty years. He is an outstanding businessman who loves the outdoors. Everyone appreciates his capacity to size up a business situation quickly, assess the pros and cons, and the decisively act, usually leading to great results.

Having traveled the almost two hours to the safari after landing, Steve and I had scrambled into our hunting gear, made sure our rifles were zeroed in, paired up with our guides, and headed out. We hadn't gotten thirty minutes into the country, grinding up a steep road, when our guide, Gary, pressed on the brakes, and exclaimed, "Jump out! Hurry!"

Grabbing our guns, we clambered out of the truck—Steve from the front, I from the back. The guide quickly directed our attention to a ridge about 150 yards away. It rose in a rather steep incline scattered with brush and sage, ruggedly rock-strewn. And just up a jagged game trail on the ridgeline strode a massive waterbuck, moving from the heavily tree-canopied lower area to the ridgeline, where in a matter of moments he would duck over the edge and be gone.

Gary excitedly instructed Steve, "Take the shot! You're not going to find a better animal than that! But be fast about it, or he's gone."

As I waited to hear the explosion of the shot, I was met with only silence. I cut a quick glance at Steve, and saw that he hadn't even shouldered his gun. My glance darted back to the monster meandering his way up the path.

I started raising my own gun, but just as quickly told myself,

"No—this needed to be Steve's shot. This was his first trip; I'd been here before." I looked at Steve, shot a glance back at the buck, then heard Gary exclaim again, "Hurry . . . shoot!"

"But a waterbuck isn't on my list," Steve answered back.

Aaaaa! Watching those massive horns crest the ridge line and disappear over the other side, my heart sank. I wished I had taken the shot myself, because he was a bruiser. And I knew, with time, Steve would wish he had as well.

For five and a half days we hunted hard over thousands and thousands of hectares of South African terrain. Steve and his two adult sons got some great animals. But he didn't see another trophy like that first-day waterbuck. To this day I'm convinced it would have been listed in the record books. Our guide would later say it was probably one of the largest he had ever seen.

I've asked myself many times, "Why didn't I jerk my rifle to my shoulder and squeeze the trigger?" But I had greatly wanted Steve to get the first shot. And somehow, I imagined that life would freeze-frame, we'd have more time, and one of us would get the shot off.

But life doesn't typically work that way. It doesn't freeze the time frames. It doesn't come with instant replays. Opportunities appear, and then they're gone. That's why we must be ready "in season and out of season"—when it's convenient and when it's not, when we are perfectly ready and when we aren't. Opportunities are fleeting, and then they are gone.

And while this is definitely true of hunting, it's also true in so much of life. It applies to areas such as our opportunities to express appreciation and love, to ask for forgiveness, or to offer a hand of help. The same thing goes with talking to someone about Christ and how they can know Him in a personal relationship. Or to ask, "Could I take a moment and pray for you right now?"

Or to share a verse of Scripture that's relevant to the need of the moment. Or to call someone on the phone when their name or face keeps popping into your mind repeatedly, and you're not sure why.

Just recently, I was on another trip with Steve, and we were discussing what lessons we had taken away from that great hunt. With a sheepish smile, Steve said, "To listen . . . and act . . . when your guide gives you direction."

That's a great lesson in hunting, as well as in following Christ. When He impresses on our mind and heart to act, that is *exactly* what we should do—and the very moment we should do it! Not later. Acting within the moment the impression comes—that is obedience. And that is what God has promised He will honor.

⊕ Taking Aim

1. When was the last time you felt an impression to do something, didn't do it, and were sorry later?

2. What has God impressed you to do in recent times, which you haven't followed through on, but which it may *not* be too late to do? What steps do you need to take to get it done?

- - -

Lord, I'm letting You define my to-do list.

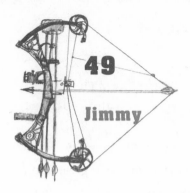

49

Jimmy

FINISH STRONG

Can you fathom the mysteries of God? Can you probe the limits of the Almighty? (Job 11:7)

The filming on the North Island of New Zealand was the stuff of a TV producer's dream. The conditions were perfect. The hunting was amazing. The people on the trip were justly suited for the adventure. Everyone was healthy and having a blast.

I couldn't have been happier, even as my wife and I hugged everyone goodbye. Our North Island experience had left us with three exciting episodes for *Spiritual Outdoor Adventures*. And my anticipation for Part Two of our quest—a tahr hunt on the South Island—was bursting inside me as we headed for the Wellington airport.

That's when the wrinkle hit.

Our daughter Christin and our unofficially adopted daughter Mary called to deliver the bad news: their mutual friend, only eighteen years of age, had passed away. She had been hanging on by a thread for several weeks after being severely injured in a fire, and had finally succumbed to the inevitable.

This young lady had been in our home on several occasions. She was such a beautiful girl. And the news of her death resounded in my ears like a hammer beating on a concrete wall. Christin and Mary cried over the phone as they told us the news. I tried to console them from halfway around the world. It was a tough moment, and the bitter taste from it still lingers in my mouth.

I don't understand why the young must die.

Like you, I've asked this question many times. I asked it about the fourteen-year-old boy who was hunting with his father in the woods behind the church where my own father preaches. As my dad was winding down his sermon one Sunday morning, ambulance and police sirens began pulling into the church parking lot. The boy's father had mistaken his son for a deer and had accidently shot him, killing him.

Decades earlier at a deer camp near Warren, Arkansas, a similar thing happened. A little boy was sitting on the edge of a power line, holding a shotgun loaded with slugs and buckshot. He was leaning against a tree and not wearing anything orange. When he pulled out a candy bar and unwrapped it to eat it, a hunter not far away saw the flash of white, and he shot. *Bang!* The bullet took the life of that little boy.

Again, I don't understand why the young sometimes die and don't live out what seem to be their full days. But I do know this: in the middle of all the loss, hurt, pain, and grief that we deal with on earth, God is already at work to make everything right in the end.

There is more to what we see than what we see.

To all our questions, He is the answer.

And while life on this earth will always mean the young must occasionally die, it also means that many of us will live on. Why isn't it just as necessary a question, then, to ask what we will do with the life that remains, though equally not ours to protect from death?

My answer: I want to finish strong.

I believe in God. I consider myself one of His own, adopted by Him, solely because of His love and not my credentials. I believe He cares. I believe He walks with me on a daily basis and delights in providing for me. I have enjoyed so many blessings, far more than any man deserves. I was even allowed to marry an angel! I have been blessed with wonderful children, amazing parents, and loyal friends who truly love me.

I daily thank God for His grace that is sufficient to cover all my sins, faults, weaknesses, and just my blatant stupidity at times. I love Him. I want to learn to love Him more. And even amid the death of our young friend, I *still* love Him, assured He knows things that I do not. So I choose to trust Him, even when I don't understand Him.

As I grow older, I recognize that the time left in my human body is fading, which leaves me feeling a hodgepodge of emotions. New struggles emerge I haven't faced before. Yet in spite of this, God is showing me more clearly than ever that my task is to finish strong. I want to stay the course. I want to expend all that I have. I want to offer all that I am. And I want to do it for the glory of God, who will make all things right in the end.

⊕ Taking Aim

1. As a general rule, the death of a young person is never in vain. For example, the death of the little boy killed along the power line in southern Arkansas caused such a stir that the hunter orange safety law

was implemented throughout the state. Many lives have been saved as a result of that action. Can you think of other positives that sometimes result from seemingly needless tragedy?

2. Read Acts 3:17–21. What promise can you claim from this passage that addresses untimely death or any other tragic occurrence?

3. 1 Peter 5:10 reports, "And the God of all grace, who called you to his eternal glory in Christ, after you have suffered a little while, will himself restore you and make you strong, firm and steadfast." What encouragement can you draw from this?

4. Even though you may not understand the mysteries of God, do you intend to follow Him all the days of your life? If so, what is your game plan for finishing strong?

- - -

Lord, help me finish. Strong.

50

Bob

WHAT'S YOUR GOAL?

Therefore I urge you, brothers, in view of God's mercy, to offer your bodies as a living sacrifice, holy and pleasing to God—this is your true and proper worship. (Romans 12:1)

It was very nearly the perfect setting. Sprawling out on the leather couches and chairs inside a Texas hunting lodge with two great friends—that's about as good as it gets, at least for me. The deer were still in rut. The weather was crisp and clear, cold enough in the morning that you could see the fog of your breath through your cupped hands. One of my friends had already taken an eight-point buck sporting marvelous tines, and he was basking in his victory.

The fire was roaring. The big-screen TV was dancing with action. And our bellies were groaning from the great dinner we had just consumed. Each of us had loosened our belts to release the building tension at our waistlines.

As our discussion picked up energy, we began talking about the rest of our lives—the parts between now and our final days on earth. What did we intend to do with them?

Jerry runs a TV network in the Midwest. Bud is a land developer and outstanding businessman. Both successful. Both men's men. And both in love with Christ, wanting to make a significant difference that will outlive their lives. As am I. And at sixty-five, fifty-nine, and fifty-five (at the time), we each felt confident, given good health and God's blessing, that we still had a long way to go before the finish line. What then are the keys to making these crucial, upcoming years count?

We talked about many of these—*focus* and *intentionality* among them. Then suddenly, Jerry stopped us in our tracks by proclaiming, "We need to be asking ourselves, 'Do we want to do something significant for God, or do we want to become more like Christ?' The answer to that statement, I believe, will make all the difference."

His comment sparked a lively and lengthy conversation. We decided that most people (yes, even Christ-followers) want to do something great *for* God, much more than they focus on *becoming more like* Christ.

Why is this the case? Could it be that we find it actually easier to *do something for* rather than to *become more like*? The first simply requires action and effort; the other requires transformation. With the first, I can remain who I am and just try harder. With the second, I must transparently hear from God and others, deciding that I need to change, which may be the hardest work of all. Not to mention, the most threatening.

The clearest sign of this discrepancy is the vast number of church-related people who confuse *busyness* with *godliness*. And the two are very different. Another way to say it is: "*Being* is more important than *doing*."

I thought back to growing up around the church and often feeling confused by the messages I was hearing. They seemed to be often worded around a well-meaning challenge of *becoming more*, yet many of the expectations, announcements, and illustrations were translated in the language of *attending* more, *volunteering* more, *giving* more, *studying* more, *going* more. You get the picture.

Could it be that the church has at times given a mixed message? Oh, not necessarily intentionally. Most likely, very unintentionally. But the church can come up with so many activities to keep going, so many events to staff, so much attendance to grow, so much money to raise. And on and on it goes.

Looking back on my journey, I can see how I very often found myself measuring my spirituality by my activity, or by my lack of it. If I desired to feel a bit more committed as a Christian, I just started trying to do more—attend more church meetings, write more checks, volunteer to help more. These days, however, I just shake my head at how mistaken I was. I confused activity with spirituality. And I discovered firsthand what a deceptive and numbing trap that can be.

So there we were, enjoying each other's camaraderie and company in a hunting lodge in deer season in the cold month of December, while also hearing one of the most insightful challenges we had ever heard, including the many challenges we'd heard before in church. It was a great reminder that God speaks to us at the most amazing times in the midst of the most unexpected circumstances. And if we aren't listening—both inside and outside the church—we are likely to miss some life-changing messages.

So which is it for you—*doing* or *becoming*? And how can you keep it in the right balance?

 Taking Aim

1. What is one thing that you feel would help you become more like Christ six months from now than you are today?

2. How do you keep *transformation* and *action* in balance so it's not *either/or* but *both/and*? And how can you be sure your action flows *out* of your transformation, and doesn't just substitute for it?

- - -

Lord, change my heart, not just my calendar.

Your Harvest Record

You probably have an old photo with words written with a sharpie on some part of the picture. Most likely it is of you with a white-tail buck or a gobbler or some other trophy that you harvested. Most likely you put the date on the photo, along with where you were and a description of the trophy (how many points, weight, weapon used). These photos can be found all over the country hanging in hunting camps, framed on desktops and shelves, or secured in photo albums. These are great reminders of wonderful life moments. Though the colors in the images may fade with time, the memories last for a lifetime.

This book that you have read is somewhat like a photo that has been printed. It is an adventure that you have shared with us, and we thank you for going on the trip through these pages with us. The possibility does exist that you might not have been a follower of Christ when you started the journey. If that has changed during your adventure through these pages, why not take a moment to write down the details in a letter and insert it here in this book. Consider this letter as the trophy photo of your adventure—and your eternal salvation is the trophy. Who knows, some day in the future when you are long gone, one of your kids, grandkids, or great-grandkids may pick up this book and look through it. Imagine their joy when they find a personal note from you about your own salvation. It might just change their life. What a trophy!